GOD'S COVERING

Moving from Glory to Glory!

ANTHONY C. BURRIS

XULON PRESS

Xulon Press
555 Winderley Pl, Suite 225
Maitland, FL 32751
407.339.4217
www.xulonpress.com

xulon PRESS

© 2024 by Anthony C. Burris

All rights reserved solely by the author. The author guarantees all contents are original and do not infringe upon the legal rights of any other person or work. No part of this book may be reproduced in any form without the permission of the author.

Due to the changing nature of the Internet, if there are any web addresses, links, or URLs included in this manuscript, these may have been altered and may no longer be accessible. The views and opinions shared in this book belong solely to the author and do not necessarily reflect those of the publisher. The publisher therefore disclaims responsibility for the views or opinions expressed within the work.

Unless otherwise indicated, Scripture quotations taken from the New King James Version (NKJV). Copyright © 1982 by Thomas Nelson, Inc. Used by permission. All rights reserved.

Scripture quotations taken from the English Standard Version (ESV). Copyright © 2001 by Crossway, a publishing ministry of Good News Publishers. Used by permission. All rights reserved.

Scripture quotations taken from the Amplified Bible (AMP). Copyright © 1954, 1958, 1962, 1964, 1965, 1987 by The Lockman Foundation. Used by permission. All rights reserved.

Scripture quotations taken from the Holy Bible, New Living Translation (NLT). Copyright ©1996, 2004, 2007 by Tyndale House Foundation. Used by permission of Tyndale House Publishers, Inc.

Paperback ISBN-13: 978-1-66289-362-9
Ebook ISBN-13: 978-1-66289-363-6

GOD'S COVERING

Table of Contents

Introduction 5
Know Who and Whose You Are! 9
   The Creator and the Created 10
   The Journey of Transformation 15
   The Human Soul 17
   Ancestral Roots 19
   Knowing and Living in Your True Identity 34
   Recognize and Know His Voice 36
   Know Your Connections 42
   Know Your Value 44
Know Your Rights 47
   Our Covenant with God 50
   Jesus Christ Our Advocate & High Priest 54
   Access to the Father (the Only Sovereign God) 59
   Your Teacher, Counselor, & Seal of Approval
   (Holy Spirit) 62
   Your Right to Remain Silent: Be Still and Know 66
God's Divine Covering 71
   The Defeated Accuser 79
Embrace Your Worship of God! 86
   Growing in Prayer Worship 90
   Growing in His Grace, Purpose, & Assignment 96

Embrace Your Freedom! 104

One God, One Body, & One Spirit! 115

Lifelong Application. 124

Eat Well and Exercise!. 127

Some Names of God & Helpful Terms 132

Some Common Terms 134

References 136

Prelude

The scripture declares that "He who dwells in the secret place of the Most-High Shall abide under the shadow of the Almighty" (Ps. 91:1 NKJV). The word used in this scripture for secret place means a covering or to hide by covering. (H5643 Strongs Concordance) It speaks of concealing, protecting, and keeping close. We will read throughout this book how God's will from the beginning has been to cover us with His glory.

The word **covering** speaks of something that covers or conceals. Therefore, a covering is a means of providing protection, a way to guard against attacks and for one to afford the protection of security against loss. Covering is also a way to conceal by putting something out of sight. We can think of a bride who covers herself in beautiful white garments with a veil over her face, concealing her beauty for only her husband to unveil.

God's covering provides all these things to the believer. We are the bride of Christ, and our white garment is His righteousness covering us. His provision of salvation is our protection against evil and the security of eternal life in Jesus Christ. His covering dispatches Father's army of angelic protection. His covering affords us the riches of His kingdom, protecting us from lack.

He makes Himself a banner over His people, declaring to all creation that we are His own special people. He invites us into His secret place—His covering—for us to abide under His defense. Jesus echoes the love of the Father, declaring how often He wanted to gather us as a hen gathers her chicks under her wings.

The scriptures declare how the Father guided His people by spreading a cloud of covering by day and providing fire to give light in the night. His call is to the whole world to come under His covering and be clothed with His glory. The scripture says, "For God so loved the world that He gave His only begotten Son, that whoever believes in Him should not perish but have everlasting life" (John 3:16 NKJV).

The Father gave us Jesus Christ to be our covering and restore us to His glory. And not only us, but the provision is there for all, for whoever will receive Him. It is the Father's will for the whole earth to be full of His glory. The prophet Isaiah declares to us God's will for His people. Consider the scriptures below.

> "And one cried to another and said: 'Holy, holy, holy is the Lord of hosts; The whole earth is full of His glory!'" (Isa. 6:3 NKJV).

> "O Lord, I will honor and praise your name, for you are my God. You do such wonderful things! You planned them long ago, and now you have accomplished them. But you are a tower of refuge

to the poor, O Lord, a tower of refuge to the needy in distress. You are a refuge from the storm and a shelter from the heat. For the oppressive acts of ruthless people are like a storm beating against a wall, or like the relentless heat of the desert. But you silence the roar of foreign nations. As the shade of a cloud cools relentless heat, so the boastful songs of ruthless people are stilled. In Jerusalem, the Lord of Heaven's Armies will spread a wonderful feast for all the people of the world. It will be a delicious banquet with clear, well-aged wine and choice meat. There he will remove the cloud of gloom, the shadow of death that hangs over the earth. He will swallow up death forever! The Sovereign Lord will wipe away all tears. He will remove forever all insults and mockery against his land and people. The Lord has spoken! In that day the people will proclaim, 'This is our God! We trusted in him, and he saved us! This is the Lord, in whom we trusted. Let us rejoice in the salvation he brings!'" (Isa. 25:1, 4–9 NLT).

These scriptures speak of a time when all the earth will be full of God's glory. Father will throw a banquet for all the nation, and the people will sit down together without fear or biases. In that day, there will be no more crying, and death will have no more power to take lives. All the peoples will trust in the LORD our God. Until then, we are all work in progress, being transformed into the image of Christ.

Introduction

My goal and purpose are to share what I believe God has given to me. It is my prayer that those reading this book will comprehend the love and provisions of the Father. It is the Father's will for us to be covered with His glory. He has declared that the whole earth will be full of His glory. I have found that there is a gap in the development of the believer after coming into relationship with Christ and in teaching them the full counsel of God to sustain their successful growth. The scriptures command us to be about "teaching them to observe all things that I have commanded you . . ." (Matt. 28:20)

When I first gave my life to Christ, at fifteen years old, and got baptized, that was the end of any further discussion or outreach to me by the church. For whatever reasons, there must have been a lack of interest once I made the steps of receiving Christ. There was no one to teach, mentor, sit down with me for a Bible study, or even present me with a Bible. I just kept on living according to my old ways now that I had "the get out of hell card" by giving my life to Christ. How about you? How often does anyone, such as an elder in your church, another church member, or a pastor, took the time to disciple you? Many churches have discipleship programs, but sadly, many do not spend the time to disciple believers. Too often, we go to church only to be preached at regarding our sins, what we should or should not be doing, the need for repentance, or just something motivational.

How often are you in church and can finish the pastor's message? Is it that you know so much or that you have heard it before? To be clear, there is nothing wrong with hearing the same truths over and over again. There is a song that says, "Sing them over again to me, wonderful words of life." (Church Hymnal Song #205) The apostle Peter said, "For this reason I will not be negligent to remind you always of these things, though you know and are established in the present truth. Yes, I think it is right, as long as I am in this tent, to stir you up by reminding you" (2 Pet. 1:12–13 NKJV). Therefore, it is a good thing to be reminded of the truth of God's Word and to hear things that you may have missed the first time around. But still there is a need for individual and collective training and teachings about the truth of God's Word.

As a church body, we are good at the message of salvation but often light on the teaching of the whole counsel of God. The scripture in Hebrews says, "Therefore, leaving the discussion of the elementary principles of Christ, let us go on to perfection, not laying again the foundation of repentance from dead works and of faith toward God, of the doctrine of baptisms, of laying on of hands, of resurrection of the dead, and of eternal judgment. And this we will do if God permits" (Heb. 6:1-3 NKJV).

Even these elementary principles I had to learn with the help of the Holy Spirit on my own. Yes, there were messages preached on these topics and there were a few bible studies but many things I had to learn through my own studies and experiences. I'm not here to offer some deep insightful "meat" that many seasoned Christian do not know. But I believe there is a gap in the teaching of the newborn in Christ, that same gap of lacking knowledge and understanding that I had fallen into. Therefore, this book is a means of conveying even some of those elementary principles to the unchurched, the wavering Christian, and the newborn who may not be getting that teaching.

I know that I am guilty of abandoning some of those who I have personally led to Christ. I have been working in my assignment as a teacher in the NYC school system for over thirty-five years. I've helped many along the way to Christ and some who were already in Christ. However, I have not had a lot of opportunity to help them grow to maturity in Christ.

Many times, we lead someone to Christ, and we then invite them to church or tell them to find a good Bible-preaching church, or we do something along these lines.

I have always wanted to do something more to be sure that the new believer or maturing Christian not only have a strong foundation but grow to a level of maturity that they can remain in Christ no matter where they go. The apostle Paul puts it this way, "My little children, for whom I labor in birth again until Christ is formed in you . . ." (Gal. 4:19--20 NKJV).

Is there anyone for whom you have labored for them to come to know Christ but now have doubts if they are still living for Christ? It is Father's will that our fruit should remain. We must labor again, if necessary, until Christ is formed in them. For this reason, I am writing this book in hopes of helping to establish some foundation in the lives of those who may be on the fence, struggling to understand, and for those who have recently given their lives to Christ and want a deeper understanding of who they are in Christ and the provisions Father have established to help us in every step of our sojourn.

Know Who and Whose You Are!

We were all born into this world under various circumstances. Some of us are the result of a loving relationship, some are fatherless, some are adopted, some were carried by surrogates, some are the result of incest, and still others from rape. It's important to understand that we are loved by God no matter what our beginnings may be. The scriptures say that even when your mother and father forsake you, the Lord will take care of you (Ps. 27:10).

All of us have our own stories, and each of us has experienced varying degrees of success, abuse, abandonment, failure, and all the struggles of living. By no means does this mean that God wasn't there and didn't send you help in your situation. God has committed the care of this world to mankind, and He often does His work through people. The people used by God are not always Christians nor even believers. God, in His wisdom and power, will move even the heart of an atheist to fulfill His will to cover us with His glory and perfect us in Christ. The scriptures say that even "The king's heart is in the hand of the Lord, Like the rivers of water; He turns it wherever

He wishes" (Prov. 21:1 NKJV). Therefore, He can use even our enemies to fulfill His purposes for our lives.

So, what do all these things have to do with who you are? Let us first have a look at how and why we were created.

The Creator and the Created

God our Creator made us in His image. God is Spirit, and therefore His image is not physical. His image is the attributes He possesses. For example, He is the eternally sovereign God Who rules over all His creation. Therefore, He created us to live forever and have dominion over all the earth. The first commandment given to us is to be caretakers of over the Earth. We were to accomplish this by remaining in obedience and fellowship with God.

Man made the choice to disobey God, and that disobedience resulted in two major changes. Prior to Adam and Eve's willful disobedience, they had divine authority over all the earth. They needed no garments to cover their bodies. They had access to the tree of life. As long as they obeyed God, they experienced no pains, bloodsheds, sufferings, nor death. The Father had them covered with His glory. As soon as they disobeyed God's command, they became separated from God and subjects of Death. Mankind lost the glory and covering of God. They became servants of the one who deceived them, Satan, who was operating through the serpent. See Genesis 1–2 for greater details.

God could no longer fellowship with mankind the way He fellowship with them prior to their fall of disobedience. But God had a plan to redeem mankind from death to life, and He told Satan operating through the serpent that "the Seed" of the woman would bruise his head. That Seed is the promised Seed of Abraham through whom it was promised that all the nations will be blessed. That Seed is "The Son of God," who was given and was eventually born through the Virgin Mary. This Son of God is Jesus the Christ. He is also called Immanuel, meaning God with us. In other words, God orchestrated a way to reconcile mankind back to Himself by taking on the form of a man.

The mission of Jesus was, first and foremost, to be completely obedient to the Father. Through His complete obedience, He overcame Satan, sin, and the sufferings of death on the cross in order that mankind would be reconciled with God. This is the unmeasurable love of God for mankind, that the Son of God would leave His glory to put on sinful flesh, endure sufferings like we do, and then lay down His life on the cross so that we can be reconciled to God and have eternal life.

> *For God so loved the world that He gave His only begotten Son, that whoever believes in Him should not perish but have everlasting life. For God did not send His Son into the world to condemn the world, but that the world through Him might be saved.* (John 3:16–17 NKJV).

In light of all that God our Creator, through Jesus Christ, has done to reconcile us back to Himself, what will your response to His love be? Jesus Christ, the only begotten Son of God, was incarnated into this world in order for you and me to be saved. You see, those who receive Him as Lord and Savior have the right to become children of God. They will not come into judgment and have passed from the power of death into life. There's no longer any condemnation for those who are abiding in Christ. Jesus said, "Most assuredly, I say to you, he who hears My word and believes in Him who sent Me has everlasting life, and shall not come into judgment, but has passed from death into life" (John 5:24 NKJV).

Those who refuse this gift of life is already condemned from the beginning because of our actions, those of our forefathers. Those who choose not to be reconciled with God through Jesus Christ is, by this very action, aligning themselves with Satan. A problem with aligning with Satan is that he is already judged and awaiting sentencing. A place of punishment is prepared for him and all his allies, a place of eternal punishment.

Jesus spoke about hell quite often, and this is a good place to address this topic. When the scriptures talk about hell, it is usually in reference to two places: Hades, the place of everlasting punishment or the place of departed souls, and the lake of fire, which is the place of eternal punishment. These places were not created for mankind; they were created for the punishment of Satan and his fallen angels. However, when mankind aligned themselves with Satan, they fall under the same judgment and punishment.

The good news is that God, through Jesus Christ, paid the penalty of our sins. There is no need for us to suffer the wrath of God, which was meant for Satan and his followers. The cost of our salvation was accomplished by Jesus on the cross when He said, "It is finished," (John 19:30) and bowed His head, giving up His life so that we can have eternal life. But more importantly, He rose from the grave on the third day, stripping Death and Hades of their power. Because Jesus Christ lives eternally, those who are in Christ will also live eternally. Consider the following scriptures, and may God grant you understanding.

> *"I am He who lives, and was dead, and behold, I am alive forevermore. Amen. And I have the keys of Hades and of Death"* (Rev. 1:18 NKJV).

> *"So, when this corruptible has put on incorruption, and this mortal has put on immortality, then shall be brought to pass the saying that is written: 'Death is swallowed up in victory.' 'O Death, where is your sting? O Hades, where is your victory?' The sting of death is sin, and the strength of sin is the law. But thanks be to God, who gives us the victory through our Lord Jesus Christ"* (1 Cor. 15:54–57 NKJV).

It is not very difficult to take the step of faith to receive Christ, but it is the most important decision any of us will ever make. You do not start out by knowing everything, but I've given you plenty to think about. Knowing who you are is the key to unlocking all the rights, privileges, and responsibilities that are available to you as a child of God. It begins with this first right, "as many as received Him, to them **He gave the right to become children of God**, to those who believe in His name" (John 1:12 NKJV Emphasis added).

If you believe and want to put your faith in God through Jesus Christ, then start by praying this prayer:

> *Father in heaven and Sovereign God, you are holy and worthy of all praises, all honor, and all glory forever! Your will be done, and Your kingdom come on earth as in heaven. Today I ask you for the gift of Your bread of life. I ask Your forgiveness for all my sins and disobedience in the name of Jesus Christ. Help me to forgive those who have done wrongs to me just as You have forgiven me. For to You belong the kingdom, the power, and the glory. I belong to You, and I receive Your Son Jesus Christ as my Lord and Savior. I commit my life to obeying Your Word daily; help me to place my trust in You. Thank you, Father, for Your gift of salvation and eternal life in Christ Jesus. Amen!*

The Journey of Transformation

Now that you have received Jesus Christ, what happens next? Well, a good starting point would be to share your faith with a trusted pastor, friend in Christ or a family member. Making a public declaration that you are a follower of Christ is important and equally important is to be baptized by immersion in water. Water baptism by being immersed into water is a representation of the relinquishment of your will, your ungodly ways (death to self), and your release from any ties to Satan.

Through baptism, you identify with the death, burial, and resurrection of Jesus Christ. You are spiritually dying to this world, buried by immersion in water, and raised into a new life in Christ when you are taken up from the water. You become a new creation in Jesus Christ, your old way of life is buried, and Christ gives you a divine nature to live in right standing toward God. Although this declaration of your faith and baptism takes only a brief moment, the actual transformation from your old ways to your new nature in Christ will take some time. This is where you must make daily choices to resist your old ways, temptation, and the devil.

Instead of giving in to those things, you choose to submit to God and allow Him to complete this transformation of your life. This is called presenting yourself a living sacrifice to God.

> *"I beseech you therefore, brethren, by the mercies of God, that you present your bodies a living sacrifice, holy, acceptable to God, which is your*

> *reasonable service. And do not be conformed to this world, but be transformed by the renewing of your mind, that you may prove what is that good and acceptable and perfect will of God"* (Rom. 12:1–2 NKJV).

This transformation is not easy, especially in our current cultural environment. Also, we have a common enemy, Satan, whom the scripture says goes about like a roaring lion seeking whom he may devour. But we also know that Christ suffered likewise and was tempted in all points as we are, yet did not sin. Best of all, He has given us gifts, rights, privileges, and responsibilities to help us overcome just as He also overcame.

One of Satan's first strategies is to make you doubt your identity. He tries to make you question what God has given to you and cause you to compromise your relationship with God. It is the same thing that He did in the beginning to Eve and Adam, and then Satan tried the same thing with Jesus Christ. The scriptures tell us that after Jesus had fasted for forty days and forty nights, Satan the tempter came to test Jesus's identity. The scripture says, "Now when the tempter came to Him, he said, **"If you are the Son of God**, command that these stones become bread" (Matt. 4:3 NKJV, emphasis added).

We are living in such a time of great uncertainty, confusion of roles, and sexuality. Many of our youth are struggling with identity and sexuality issues. How many of our youth know their heritage and ancestry? How many have guiding principles and values to propel them into their destiny?

Many adults find themselves in the same dilemma of situational living. We live paycheck to paycheck and go about just existing rather than truly living. How many of us engage in toxic relationships just because we want to identify with some cause, some image of what we think life should be, or just to associate with certain individuals or groups of people? How many of us really stop and take an introspective self-analysis of who you really are: what's our purpose, and what impact do we have on our environment?

As we read in the scriptures, the devil's first attack is on our identity. If we don't know who we are, how can we truly live to our fullest potential? How do we walk into our destiny with the authority to have a lasting impact on our environment? Our enemy, Satan, knows this, and many of us have been under a constant barrage of attacks on our identity from the time of birth.

The Human Soul

We are living in a time where many people are living according to their feelings. They have confused feelings and emotions with truth and are living based on what they feel because of the pleasures produced by their feelings. I'm happy or this makes me happy is what they profess. Therefore, the happiness they feel justifies the lifestyles they choose. The sad thing is that feelings come and go, but the effects of our actions reverberate throughout our lives.

Our thoughts, emotions, and feelings are real and factual, but they are not necessarily true. Our thoughts, feelings and emotions can and often do lie to us. Our thoughts, emotions and feelings are what our soul is comprised of. We are therefore living according to the pleasures and desires of our soul. The soul is not necessarily rational and can be extremely deceptive. Because of this, we have in society those who take pleasure in lying or stealing and have no remorse. We have those who have multiple sexual relationships, simultaneously, and that makes them happy. We have those who are pedophiles lost in their perverse feelings. Our society has people engaging in all manner of behaviors, because it feels good and makes them happy.

Throughout the history of mankind, we have had those who are heterosexuals, homosexuals, Adulterers, and others practicing bestiality. Before anyone thinks I'm judging them, let me be clear in saying, I have in one way or the other experienced all of the above. I've been molested, adulterous, and coming from the country lifestyle, I've messed with animals growing up as a child. I'm not the judge of anyone. Scripture tells us that, "The heart is deceitful above all things, and desperately wicked; who can know it?" (Jer. 17:9 NKJV) Therefore, I am only saying that mankind has engaged in all sought of behaviors, in the pursuit of happiness and power.

The soul can be insatiable, and if we live only by our thoughts, feelings, and emotions, there is no ending to the depths of depravity mankind could experience. We must have a standard, a means of measuring our thoughts, feelings, and emotions, to guard against depravity. While we cannot deny our feelings and emotions, we must not allow only these to dictate our happiness or standards of living. We must have a ruler, an absolute measure to guide our standards of living. I believe that measure is truth! I also believe that the Word of God is the Truth, and that Truth is Jesus Christ.

Our history or ancestral roots can also be a guide and a measure for our current path, to avoid the errors of the past. Knowing the inherent flaws of our feelings and emotions, errors of our past including the actions of our ancestors, and also heeding the teachings of the Word of God, we can live beyond the mere pleasures and desires of our souls. We can find happiness and pleasure in life without succumbing to the dictates of the soul. We can live in the possibilities and truth of who we were created to be.

Ancestral Roots

But who are you really? Well, first of all, we're made in the image of God, the Creator of all things, for His pleasure and purpose. Since we are created beings, one of the things we need to understand is why we were created in the first place. Secondly, it may be helpful to know and understand our ancestry or the legacy of our ancestors. Thirdly, who are we connected to, and what is the basis of that connection? Scripture tells us that in the beginning, God created man in His own image; in the image of God, He created him; male and female, He created them.

And why did God create mankind? To have dominion, to rule over the entire earthly realm, filling the earth with His glory.

> "Then God said, 'Let Us make man in Our image, according to Our likeness; let them have dominion over the fish of the sea, over the birds of the air, and over the cattle, over all the earth and over every creeping thing that creeps on the earth.' So, God created man in His own image; in the image of God, He created him; male and female He created them" (Gen. 1:26-27 NKJV)

> "Blessed be the Lord God, the God of Israel, who only does wondrous things! And blessed be His glorious name forever! And let the whole earth be filled with His glory. Amen and Amen" (Ps. 72:18–19 NKJV).

> "Then the Lord said: "I have pardoned, according to your word; but truly, as I live, all the earth shall be filled with the glory of the Lord" (Num. 14:20–21 NKJV).

The image of God is not the physical form in which we behold mankind. God is Spirit, and thus He created mankind as spiritual beings endowed with the attributes of God. We were, in essence, clothed in the glory of God and were to fill the earth and subdue it with His glory. But the scriptures record that the devil, whom mankind was supposed to subdue, working through the serpent, deceived man into giving up the glory and authority that God had endowed them with.

Because we fell into the deception of that old serpent, we have all lived in the sin of disobedience to God and have thereby shrouded our identity under the deceptive power of the devil. We have all sinned and fallen short of the glory of God. But like a good father and parent, God has made it His mission, His will, to rescue, restore, and reconcile us back to Himself. It is His will that we, once again, be covered with and filled with His glory. Therefore, from the beginning, He, in His foreknowledge of each of us, decided to reconcile us to Himself. God has a plan for every one of us individually and collectively. He has made the way for our reconciliation and is actively working on our behalf for our restoration.

What does it mean to be reconciled to God through Christ? How does this clarify who I am? In short, there are two considerations to this question. The first is reflected in the story of the prodigal son. Like this son who left the father to live a sinful life, we became dead to God and alienated from the family of God. Like the son in this parable was restored to sonship, when we are reconciled to God through Christ, we are also restored to a position of royalty. (See Luke 15:11–32). Consider verses 20 to 24 of the passage and the points that follows below.

> *And he arose and came to his father. But when he was still a great way off, his **father saw him***

and had compassion, and ran and fell on his neck and kissed him. And the son said to him, "Father, I have sinned against heaven and in your sight, and am no longer worthy to be called your son." But the father said to his servants, **"Bring out the best robe and put it on him and put a ring on his hand and sandals on his feet.** And bring the fatted calf here and kill it and let us eat and be merry; for this my son was dead and is alive again; he was lost and is found.' And they began to be merry" (Luke 15:11–24 NKJV, emphasis added).

The Father Ran

This shows compassion, grace, mercy, forgiveness, and reconciliation. Father saw us and had compassion while we were still a great way off! Before we were even able to confess our sins, the Father embraced us and kissed us. He reconciled us to Himself, knowing already what was in our hearts. Then we were able to confess our sins and receive forgiveness! This is representative of how we are saved by grace.

Note that when the Father saw him afar off, the Father had compassion on him. How many of us parents would have been angry or bitter? Might we have rather said, "Go back to where you're coming from!"? Perhaps we would not have even been open to speak to this child who was dead to us after running off with his inheritance and wasting it. But God, the Father, had compassion and showed grace. The good Father received His son as one resurrected from a dead state of being. This was not a process of watching to see changes in the son first. It was immediate acceptance and reconciliation to sonship as one who was no longer dead but raised to life. The dead works of the son was never mentioned, nor was he repudiated for his actions. The good Father showed grace even before there was transformation.

Robe of Righteousness

The Father instructed His servants to bring out the best robe and put it on him! Jesus, the Servant of God, washed and sanctified us, then clothed us with His righteousness so that we could live in the presence of Father for eternity. All provisions were given to the prodigal son to restore him to sonship, dwelling with the father.

In the Father's kingdom, there is no need to go about building your own kingdom. To do so is an act of rebellion, which is what the prodigal son had done by leaving his father's house. The Father has already made provisions for us to be clothed in righteousness. He has prepared a place for us. He has a plan for our lives. The independence we experience in this country drives us away from our heritage in a futile quest to create and establish our own thing. This makes it difficult for us to receive the provisions Father has already put in place for His children. We can live in righteousness because He has already covered us with His righteousness.

Our own self-righteousness is like filthy rags before the Father. When we humble ourselves to receive the provisions of the Father, then we can enjoy true freedom from dead works and enjoy life in the Son of His love. Dead works or dead things cannot produce nor impart life! We must receive life from the Father, and His life will multiply in and through us. The scripture says, "This my son was dead and is now alive again." Also consider the following scriptures.

> "The scripture says, 'He has delivered us from the power of darkness and conveyed us into the kingdom of the Son of His love, in whom we have redemption through His blood, the forgiveness of sins'" (Col. 1:13-14 NKJV).

Ring of Restoration and Authority

The family seal, a ring, was placed on his hand! The Servant: Christ also gave us the Family Seal, who is the Holy Spirit! He is in us for all eternity; never will He leave us nor forsake us! The Holy Spirit is our seal of approval that we are children of the Most-High God and are part of the family in heaven.

In the old days, families, especially royal families, had a family crest. It was a signet that established the fact that you were a part of a certain family or clan. Today, the same concept is used with family names or last names. Also, in current times, we use other things, such as sororities, trademarks, tattoos, or even colors to show that we belong to certain groups.

In the final days, Satan will also put his mark on his followers. But God's family seal will be placed within and upon all who belong to Him.

Before continuing with the story of the prodigal son, let us consider the second point of understanding who we are and our purposes by discussing our Heavenly family. As I said, we should consider the legacy of our ancestors, but to do so, we must address the issue of family, and who are our ancestors?

Family can be a very touchy subject for some people, so let us focus on the biblical concepts of family. Even as Jesus was laying down His life on the cross, the scriptures records that his biological (earthly) and spiritual (heavenly) family were present in support of Him. The scriptures also record how Jesus blended the two families by assigning the apostle John to become a standing son to Jesus's mother Mary. Consider this scripture below.

> "Now there stood by the cross of Jesus His mother, and His mother's sister, Mary the wife of Clopas, and Mary Magdalene. When Jesus therefore saw His mother, and the disciple whom He loved standing by, He said to His mother, 'Woman, behold your son!' Then He said to the disciple, 'Behold your mother!' And from that hour that disciple took her to his own home" (John 19:25–27 NKJV).

We grow up hearing that blood is thicker than water! This is usually said to express the fact that family ties are or at least should be stronger than any other relationship ties. But if you've lived long enough, you know that's not always the truth for many families. One other thing that's often said is that, in the end, all you have is your family, referring to biological family. Again, in this saying, there is truth, but not in all situations.

Jesus taught us that our strongest relationship ties should be between our Heavenly family. I know that this is a difficult and strong statement, especially for those who have been church hurt. But let's remember that Jesus was also church hurt. So many of the religious leaders did not believe nor welcomed Him. Many, even from His own town, didn't believe him, and we know He was betrayed by one of His own disciples who ate from His very hand. Yet, He strongly insisted that His brothers and sisters were those who did the will of His Father in Heaven.

However, Jesus also valued blood relationships. We can see in the above scripture that at the moment of His death on the cross, Christ had those who were close to Him standing at the foot of the cross. I believe this may be the only place that His aunt, the sister of His mother, is ever mentioned in the Bible. But here at His moment of death, there were biological and spiritual family members. Also note that as the older son, Jesus was still concerned with taking care of His widowed mother, Mary, and appointed His close spiritual son to take His place in caring for His biological mother. This is a reminder that we all have a responsibility to care for our biological family as much as our spiritual family. This responsibility is obvious by the actions of Christ and the commandment to honor our father and mother. The commandment is to honor both parents and not just the mothers.

What else did Christ say about family? There was the time when His brothers and mother came to see him while He was teaching his disciples.

> *Then His brothers and His mother came, and standing outside they sent to Him, calling Him. And a multitude was sitting around Him; and they said to Him, "Look, your mother and Your brothers are outside seeking You." But He answered them, saying, "Who is My mother, or My brothers?" And He looked around in a circle at those who sat about Him, and said, "Here are My mother and My brothers! For whoever does the will of God is My brother and My sister and mother"* (Mark 3:31–35 NKJV).

Even after His resurrection from the dead, He continued to reassure His disciples that God the Father was not just His Father but also our Father and God. Prior to His death and resurrection, He taught the disciples to pray, saying, "Our Father Who is in Heaven . . ." Now after His resurrection, He again made the point of telling the disciples who their Father was. Jesus spoke to Mary Magdalene, giving her a message to report to his disciples.

> *"Jesus said to her, 'Do not cling to Me, for I have not yet ascended to My Father; but go to My brethren and say to them,* **"I am ascending to My Father and your Father, and to My God and your God"'"** (John 20:17 NKJV).

Jesus teaches us that our concept of family should go beyond just biological and must include those who are doing the will of our Father in Heaven. This is an expanded and more accurate description of how Father sees family. God doesn't only focus on biological; He also looks at behavior, which is an outward showing of who we really are inside. In other words, the fruit of our actions is a result of whose seed is within us. So, if you are family, start living like it; start producing the fruit of the Spirit of God.

Look at the example of Cain and Abel; was Cain a brother to Abel? No! He murdered Abel; although by blood, they were family, by spirit, Cain was of the seed of the serpent while Abel was of a righteous seed, and even from the ground, his blood cried out to God and was heard. Examine the scripture below also and see how Jesus dealt with the ancestors of Abraham who were not living like Abraham.

> *"I know that you are Abraham's descendants, but you seek to kill Me, because My word has no place*

in you. I speak what I have seen with My Father, and you do what you have seen with your father." They answered and said to Him, "Abraham is our father." Jesus said to them, "If you were Abraham's children, you would do the works of Abraham. But now you seek to kill Me, a Man who has told you the truth which I heard from God. Abraham did not do this. You do the deeds of your father." Then they said to Him, "We were not born of fornication; we have one Father—God." Jesus said to them, "If God were your Father, you would love Me, for I proceeded forth and came from God; nor have I come of Myself, but He sent Me. Why do you not understand My speech? Because you are not able to listen to My word. You are of your father the devil, and the desires of your father you want to do. He was a murderer from the beginning, and does not stand in the truth, because there is no truth in him. When he speaks a lie, he speaks from his own resources, for he is a liar and the father of it. But because I tell the truth, you do not believe Me" (John 8:37–45 NKJV).

Note that although they were descendants of Abraham, Christ did not consider them to be children of Abraham because their deeds did not line up with the deeds of Abraham. When they insisted that they were not illegitimate descendants but that God was their Father, Christ said their true father was the devil because his works were what they were seeking to do in trying to kill Him and not believing the truth.

How about you? Do you believe the Truth? Are you angry at your brother without cause? What is the condition of your heart toward your brothers and sisters in Christ and even toward your biological family? It is not only your bloodline that makes you family, but, most of all, it's the fruit of your actions that shows our allegiances to either God the Father or Satan! Every tree produces its own kind of fruit; what kind of fruit are you producing? Who is your father?

The first point here is that we are family because we believe in the LORD and do the will of the Father. But we are also family because of the precious blood of Jesus Christ. Furthermore, as the spiritual bloodline of Abraham, we are called to love the LORD our Father above all and love each other as He has loved us. We cannot live with anger, bitterness, backbiting, jealousy, or secretly praying things don't work out for our brothers or sisters. Our love and actions toward each other matter to God. How we care for each other matters to God! Demonstrating love, kindness, patience, self-control, forgiveness, and godliness shows the characteristics of being children of God.

There are only two sets of families on earth!

> *In this the children of God and the children of the devil are manifest: Whoever does not practice righteousness is not of God, nor is he who does not love his brother. For this is the message that*

> *you heard from the beginning, that we should love one another, not as Cain, who was of the wicked one and murdered his brother. And why did he murder him? Because his works were evil and his brother's righteous* (1 John 3:10–12 NKJV).

Now let us get back to the story of the prodigal son. We see that Jesus, the Servant of God, reconciled us to the family of Heaven and gave us the seal of the Holy Spirit.

Restoration to Glory begins with sandals on our feet. In the next point of the prodigal son's story, we see that sandals were placed on his feet. This act, I believe, is a representation of a part of our restoration to glory, the splendor of God covering our fallen nakedness. Note that the prodigal son came back without anything on his feet, so he was exposed to the elements. He needed his feet washed and for sandals to be placed on his feet.

Jesus made a point of saying to Peter concerning the washing of his feet, "if I do not wash you, you have no share with me" (John 13:8 ESV). In other words, to be a bearer of the glory of God, our feet must be clean and covered. Father doesn't leave His children destitute. He covers them with His love, mercy, righteousness, and glory.

Even from the beginning, when mankind fell and forfeited His glory, Father killed an animal, then used the skin to cover Adam and Eve. This was a prophetic act concerning the shedding of Christ's blood for the remission of sins and the restoration of Father's covering over His children.

Although there is a crown set aside for each of us, we must go from glory to glory, and that glory also begins with, figuratively speaking, sandals on our feet. The more we abide and dwell in Him, the greater the glory. We all, starting with sandals on our feet, grow from strength to strength and from glory to glory! This is not something only for the pastor or those in leadership; it's for all God's children.

Whether you are a newborn believer like the prodigal son returning home or a seasoned apostle like Paul, His covering is for you. The covering of God is for the children of God! It is a place and position of abiding in our heavenly Father. The Father calls to all His children to come and dwell in His secret place. "He who dwells in the secret place of the Most-High Shall abide under the shadow of the Almighty" (Ps. 91:1 NKJV). He is calling all His children to come and abide, dwell in His glory.

The Responsibility of Sonship

Positionally, we are reconciled and restored, but we must grow in authority and power as we submit to the will and way of the Father. This brings us to the second point of consideration in our being reconciled to God and who we are. This point deals with the responsibility of sonship to be about the will of the Father. As stated in the scriptures, "But you are a chosen generation, a royal priesthood, a holy nation, His own special people, that you may proclaim the praises of Him who called you out of darkness into His marvelous light" (1 Pet. 2:9 NKJV).

There is so much power in this scripture, but we will focus on only three words. The first is *chosen*. You are *chosen*; I am *chosen* by God and for God. We belong to Him, and that is who we are: *chosen* children of God. We have the same mission as Jesus except for the dying for the sins of the world. In other words, we ought to be about reconciling others to God and not about judging nor condemning. Our primary mission is to spread the good news, which is focused on God's love for us all.

The second word is *royal*. We became children of the Sovereign God, the King of kings; we are, in fact, royalty. As a part of the royal family, there are privileges, promises, and responsibilities imputed to us. We have a responsibility first to the King and then to the kingdom or the subjects of the kingdom; in other words, the first two commandments: love the Lord your God above all and love each other as He has loved us. Our restoration to this position, as *royal* children of God, empowers us to carry out the duties and responsibilities of the kingdom. What are these responsibilities? To proclaim the praises of Him Who call us out of darkness and restore us to the family.

Note that the third word, which is *priesthood*, also carries the same weight of responsibility and authority. The scriptures tell us that Jesus is our eternal High Priest, and we are the royal *priesthood* under Christ Jesus. Therefore, He has sent us out the same way that the Father sent Him and with the same power and authority to carry out His will.

Let's have a closer look at the scriptures concerning God reconciling us to Himself. It reads,

> *Now all things are of God, who has reconciled us to Himself through Jesus Christ, and has given us the ministry of reconciliation, that is, that God was in Christ reconciling the world to Himself, not imputing their trespasses to them, and has committed to us the word of reconciliation. Now then, we are ambassadors for Christ, as though God were pleading through us: we implore you on Christ's behalf, be reconciled to God (2 Cor. 5:18–-20 NKJV).*

We are reconciled and chosen by God to be a part of His royal family, His own special people. And we have been granted gifts and authority to fulfill our responsibility as ambassadors reconciling others to the royal family of God.

Knowing and Living in Your True Identity

Sometimes we have doubts about who we are, especially when we have fallen short of the mark. But it's most important for us to remember that our identity comes from God, who cannot lie! His Word is truth yesterday, today, and forever. Therefore, even if we are currently not aligned with who He says we are, we only need to submit to His Word and get back in alignment.

We all have parents who disciplined us and were even disappointed with us. But no matter what happens, we are still their children, and they are still our parents. We are children of God if it be so that we have believed the testimony of Jesus Christ and have received Him as our Lord and Savior.

If you have not yet received Jesus Christ, then you are still under the deceptive power of the devil, living in the corruption that is in the world, and fulfilling the lust of the flesh. In short, those who are not in Christ are still indulging in sinful disobedience to God and have made themselves servants of the devil. But the scriptures declare that to as many as received Him, He have given them the right to become children of God.

> *"He came to His own, and his own did not receive Him. But as many as received Him, to them He gave the right to become children of God, to those who believe in His name"* (John 1:11–12 NKJV).

If you have believed in the finished work of Christ and have received Him as Lord and Savior, then you are a child of God, and you are in a covenant relationship with God the Father. This means that you belong to God! He is 100 percent committed to your relationship with Him and your salvation. Moreover, He has a plan for your life so that you will live an abundant life. (See 1 Cor. 6:20; Phil. 1:6; Jer. 29:11; John 10:10).

God our Father is fully committed to us here and in the ages to come. The scriptures say that while we were still sinners and enemies of God, Christ died for us, taking the penalty of God's wrath upon Himself so that we may have life. Not only did He die for us, but He also rose, overcoming death, and now is seated as our advocate at the right hand of God. Furthermore, as we abide in fellowship with Him, He provides daily cleansing and forgiveness of all our sins. As if that wasn't enough, He gives us the Holy Spirit of God to teach and guide us through this journey in fulfilling His will for our lives. The Holy Spirit is also the Seal of God upon all His children. This is a declaration to the realms that we are His children.

Furthermore, He is preparing a place custom designed for us and has provided us with angelic protection. He has given us gifts and hidden treasures of wisdom and knowledge.

> *Behold what manner of love the Father has bestowed on us, that we should be called children of God! Therefore, the world does not know us, because it did not know Him. Beloved, now we are children of God; and it has not yet been revealed what we shall be, but we know that when He is revealed, we shall be like Him, for we shall see Him as He is. And everyone who has this hope in Him purifies himself, just as He is pure* (1 John 3:1–3 NKJV).

Recognize and Know His Voice

We are in a season where we must know the voice of the Lord for ourselves. You cannot allow anyone else to dictate what God is saying for you to do. Other than your trusted counselor or pastor who God is assigned to you, you must learn to hear God directly. It is good to get a confirmation from others of what God is saying. But we must hear Father's voice for ourselves.

How do we fine-tune our ability to hear God? We must stop entertaining spirits or thoughts that do not originate from Father! Renew your mind, change your ways of thinking, and let the meditations of your heart be in alignment with His Word and acceptable to Him. Then you will grow to know His voice more intimately! There is a lot to be said about getting in control of our thoughts and, by implication, our voice and actions. Let's meditate on these three scriptures for a moment.

> *"You brood of vipers! How can you speak good, when you are evil? For out of the abundance of the heart the mouth speaks"* (Matt. 12:34 ESV).

> *"It is the Spirit who gives life; the flesh is no help at all. The words that I have spoken to you are spirit and life"* (John 6:63 ESV).

> *"Set your minds on things that are above, not on things that are on earth"* (Col. 3:2 ESV).

From our hearts, our inner being, we begin to hear the Spirit of God. If our hearts are full of bitterness, jealousy, sadness, and ungodly thoughts, it becomes difficult for us to hear God because our minds will also be full of these things. The voices of the world and our flesh are like static noises that interfere with the clarity of the voice of God.

Furthermore, if words are spirit and either produce death or life, what words are we listening to? Whose voice are you hearing? Are you giving heed to seducing spirits? We must take every thought captive and cast down every wicked imagination that is contrary to the Word of God. We are told to set our minds on the heavenly things of God and things that are of good report. This means that we have the authority and responsibility to control what our minds meditate upon. It's a matter of consecrating our thought processes so as to not misunderstand what Father is saying to us.

When God speaks and we hear Him clearly, then we are able to know our assignment. When you know your assignment, because you have received instructions from the Lord, do not be persuaded to do otherwise. Many times, well-intended brothers and sisters in Christ will try to have you come in alignment with what God has given them to do. They are sometimes ignorant of the fact that the eyes are not the ears, and the ears are not the feet. We are all one body in Christ but many members who often have different functions. Consider the following scriptures about a man of God and the old prophet.

> *Now an old prophet lived in Bethel. And his sons came and told him all that the man of God had done that day in Bethel. They also told to their father the words that he had spoken to the king. And their father said to them, "Which way did*

he go?" And his sons showed him the way that the man of God who came from Judah had gone. And he said to his sons, "Saddle the donkey for me." So, they saddled the donkey for him, and he mounted it. And he went after the man of God and found him sitting under an oak. And he said to him, "Are you the man of God who came from Judah?" And he said, "I am." Then he said to him, "Come home with me and eat bread." And he said, "I may not return with you, or go in with you, neither will I eat bread nor drink water with you in this place, for it was said to me by the word of the Lord, 'You shall neither eat bread nor drink water there, nor return by the way that you came.'" And he said to him, "I also am a prophet as you are, and an angel spoke to me by the word of the Lord, saying, 'Bring him back with you into your house that he may eat bread and drink water.'" But he lied to him. So, he went back with him and ate bread in his house and drank water. And as they sat at the table, the word of the Lord came to the prophet who had brought him back. And he cried to the man of God who came from Judah, "Thus says the Lord, 'Because you have disobeyed the word of the Lord and have not kept the command that the Lord your God commanded you, but have come back and have eaten bread and drunk water in the place of which he said to you,

> "Eat no bread and drink no water," your body shall not come to the tomb of your fathers.'" And after he had eaten bread and drunk, he saddled the donkey for the prophet whom he had brought back. And as he went away a lion met him on the road and killed him. And his body was thrown in the road, and the donkey stood beside it; the lion also stood beside the body. And behold, men passed by and saw the body thrown in the road and the lion standing by the body. And they came and told it in the city where the old prophet lived. And when the prophet who had brought him back from the way heard of it, he said, "It is the man of God who disobeyed the word of the Lord; therefore, the Lord has given him to the lion, which has torn him and killed him, according to the word that the Lord spoke to him" (1 Kings 13:11–26 ESV).

Learning from this example of the man of God, we see that even if a prophet should come to you and instructs you contrary to what the Lord spoke to you, do not immediately comply without first hearing from God. Seek God for confirmation and clarification if the word He gave you differs from what someone else is asking you to do. We sometimes fall into the trap of listening to man instead of God because we are truly seeking affirmation, commendation, or approbation and not just seeking confirmation of what God wants. God will use man to confirm His word to us, but we must learn to settle for affirmation, commendation, and approbation from God. Yes, we all need commendation, honor, applause, and respect at times. But when you think of it, this is mainly about satisfying our flesh because our spirit needs commendation only from God. However, our minds seek confirmation that it is God who speaks.

We must seek and be satisfied with the approval or applause that comes from God. Jesus said, "I do not receive honor from men" (John 5:41 NKJV). The Greek word translated honor is "doxa," meaning glory, honor, praise, worship, or dignity. (G1391 Strong Concordance). When we speak of affirmation, we are most often referring to "doxa," which speaks of being approved, applauded, and the act of receiving recognition.

Affirmation speaks of personal approval and validation but doesn't necessarily carry the weight of being applauded or honored. Approbation or commendation is more closely aligned to the word "doxa" used in the above scripture. Either way, we must seek our approbation, commendation, or affirmation from God and thereby seek to please Him first in all our actions and thoughts rather than trying to please man.

How do we know God is pleased with us? The scriptures record that without faith, it is impossible to please God, and it also records that faith without works is dead. (Hew. 11:6 & Jam. 2:17) So, if you hope to please God, works must be the substance of your faith. The evidence of you pleasing God may not yet be apparent, but your faith should lead you to not only contemplate what pleases God but to engage in doings the things that are pleasing to God. So now your works become the fruits of your faith and a testimony that you are pleasing to God.

Your works or actions are a testament of who you are! However, the works that you do are a reflection of the content of your heart, which consists of your thoughts and emotions. We must bring under control our emotions, and we must take control of our thoughts. This is how we guard our heart so that the issues that spring from it produces life and not death.

What does your works, your actions, and, equally as important, your thoughts testify about who you are? If you don't like the testimony of your actions, then renew your mind by the implementation or the practicing of what the Word of God says. By practicing the Word of God and submitting to the Spirit of Truth, He will develop your self-control, the fruit of the Spirit.

Know Your Connections

I remember driving home from work one evening and passing through the east New York area of Brooklyn. The traffic was very heavy, so while navigating through parked vehicles, I must have crossed over the yellow line, but so did everyone else. About two blocks down, I saw flashing lights behind me, so I pulled over. Two officers came over and demanded, "License and registration!" While I searched for my documents to give them, the officer continued, saying, "Your left tires crossed over the yellow line two blocks down on Pitkin Avenue. I responded that I wasn't aware of that and was only trying to go around the parked vehicles. They looked in my dashboard by my vehicle tags, where I kept the police card of a few detectives I knew and that my biological father knew but had given me their card. I could see the look on their faces when they realized that they couldn't just harass me because I had connections. They looked at me and said, "Never mind; drive safe." Clearly, they had no good intentions in pulling me over even though my tires, as they say, crossed the yellow line. But because of who I was connected to, their intentions could not prevail.

We belong to the Sovereign God, to Jesus Christ, who is King of kings and Lord of lords. The angel armies of God are at our service to carry out the will of Father concerning His plans for us. The scriptures declare, "The angel of the Lord encamps all around those who fear Him and delivers them. Oh, taste and see that the Lord is good; Blessed is the man who trusts in Him! Oh, fear the Lord, you, His saints! There is no want to those who fear Him" (Ps. 34:7–9 NKJV). We are now a part of and connected to the family of God and the kingdom of heaven. We should also remain in fellowship with all the saints in the body of Christ, that is, the church. As one body of believers in Christ, we are commanded to love one another as He has loved us. These are all connections that we have and should make ourselves available to each other.

It is also important to note that the church is one, or should be one, even though we don't behave as one body of believers. When we speak of "the church," it is important to understand that it refers to the entire body of Christ. The church is not just your particular denomination, nor is it your particular racial or ethnic group. The church is not a physical building created by man's hands. The church is individually and collectively human beings in whom dwells the Father, the Son, and the Holy Spirit. Everyone who has received Jesus Christ, believing that He is the Son of God incarnated in the flesh, becomes a part of the church and family of God. We the people individually and collectively are the temple of God, the body of Christ. Consider the following scripture.

> *After this I looked, and behold, a great multitude that no one could number, from every nation, from all tribes and peoples and languages, standing before the throne and before the Lamb, clothed in white robes, with palm branches in their hands, and crying out with a loud voice, "Salvation belongs to our God who sits on the throne, and to the Lamb!" And all the angels were standing around the throne and around the elders and the four living creatures, and they fell on their faces before the throne and worshiped God (Rev. 7:9–11 ESV).*

Know Your Value

A part of knowing who you are is to recognize your worth. On one of my busy early morning travels to work, the Lord spoke a word to me that I've never forgotten. This was a time that I was active in the church, also making tracks for evangelicalism, working, and, yes, a family. My travel to work in each direction is two and a half to three hours. So, on my way to the metro north train and on the train ride, I would pray and have a devotional time with God.

That morning, the Lord said to me, "do you think doing all these things is going to make Me love you more?" I was blown away by that thought and didn't fully understand what He was saying to me. But over the years, He kept showing me His unconditional love. God loves us unconditionally and steadfastly; we don't have to do anything to earn it, nor can we do anything to increase or diminish it. You and I are greatly loved and valued by God. The scriptures declare, "But God demonstrates His own love toward us, in that while we were still sinners, Christ died for us" (Rom. 5:8 NKJV). If while we were enemies to God, living in our disobedience, He sent Christ to die for us, how much value can you place on that Jesus gave His all for us?

In one of Jesus's parables, He tells the story of how the kingdom of heaven is like a treasure. And when a person discovers this treasure, they go and sell all they have and purchase the land with that treasure. This is exactly what He did for us because we are of great value to Him. Furthermore, His love for us is steadfast; it will never diminish.

Think about your most vulnerable possession; how much did you pay for it, and how much is it worth to you? Moreover, what might be the value of that possession to others? It is often said that one man's trash is another man's treasure! The value of something is in the eyes of the beholder and how much they are willing to pay for that treasure. God sent His only begotten Son, and He chose to lay down His life for us, the price of our salvation. Moreover, He rose from the dead, overcoming death, and is alive forevermore so that He can secure and enjoy His purchased possession: you and me! You are greatly loved and valued by God!

Know Your Rights

Now that you know who you truly are, that you are very well connected and greatly loved and highly valued, what does this mean for you in your current life and environment? To know and understand our rights in His kingdom, there are some fundamental concepts we must be aware of concerning the kingdom.

Most people go about life as if our physical world and bodies are all that really matters. We pretend and ignore the fact that our world is not just a physical world but also a spiritual world. Most people live as though the spiritual world or realm is of no consequence. Deep down, we all know that there is a spiritual realm and at least that we have a spirit. But because we have very little understanding of the spiritual realm, we ignore it like the elephant in the room. We should all have learned by now that ignoring a situation and pretending it doesn't exist doesn't make it less true or less important.

God does exist! In fact, His name Yehovah or Jehovah means Self-Existing. (Ex. 3:15). He simply exists and doesn't need anything outside of Himself to in any way sustain His existence. He is self-existing! Now God is Spirit! He is not a physical being. Furthermore, within God the Father, who is Elohim, there exists three primary attributes distinct within and of themselves and simultaneously collectively one, and They function as one: Elohim, Who is the Father, His Holy Spirit of Truth, Who moves in the power of God, and His Word, Who is the Son. They are distinguishable and yet simultaneously the same. Now all of this would require another book, but for reference, consider the following scriptures: Genesis 1:1–3; John 1:1–3; 1 John 5:7; Acts 1:8; and Zechariah 4:6. There are many more scriptures to consider, but this is a good start.

The devil or Satan, angels, and demons also exist, but they are all created beings. The Sovereign God created these beings for His pleasure. "For by Him all things were created that are in heaven and that are on earth, visible and invisible, whether thrones or dominions or principalities or powers. All things were created through Him and for Him. And He is before all things, and in Him all things consist" (Col. 1:16-17 NKJV).

We see that all things God created were visible—the physical world—and invisible—the spiritual world. These worlds are not mutually exclusive; they are one and the same. The universe in which we exist consists of physical and spiritual, visible and invisible, to the naked eye, and both worlds impact us. So, when the Word of God, the Son, was incarnated in bodily form as the man Jesus the Christ, the people thought He came to take care of their physical worldly needs. But in the spiritual world, there was a greater need for forgiveness, reconciliation, and freedom from the power of sin and death. He came to mitigate our sinful condition and pay the penalty for our pardon and reconciliation.

Now that we have some fundamental concepts of His kingdom, let's talk about our rights. What do all these things mean for you in your current life and environment? Here in the United States, the accused is considered innocent until proven guilty. However, in the world the Sovereign God created and governs, we all have sinned in our rebellion against the Word of God, and God's judgment is already pronounced over all of us. This is why we are subject to death even though we were created to live eternally.

Furthermore, we have an enemy, Satan, who seeks to accuse us or have us charge God with wrongdoing. We have all sinned and fallen short of the glory of God (see Rom. 3:23). This is why Jesus said, "He who believes in Him is not condemned; **but he who does not believe is condemned already**, because he has not believed in the name of the only begotten Son of God" (John 3:18 NKJV, emphasis added). Therefore, everyone who does not believe in Son of God is already condemned and awaiting sentencing.

The good news is that the Son of God has already suffered the penalty of death for all our sins and rebellious ways. And now, today, we still can receive a full sovereign substitution pardon. The Sovereign God allowed His Son to substitute for us and suffer for all our sins. All that is required is for us to agree with that substitution by receiving Christ Jesus. When this occurs, we come into certain rights under the sovereign rule of God. These rights are governed by our covenant with God: the covenant of peace.

Your Rights!

The Covenant of Peace
- Your Advocate & High Priest
- Access to the Father (the only Sovereign God)
- Your Teacher, Advocate, & Seal of Approval
- Your right to remain silent: to be still and know!

Our Covenant with God

For those who are in Christ, your life is a confession that Jesus Christ was incarnated in the flesh, suffered, and died on the cross, was buried three days in the earth, and on the third day, He rose from the dead. He now lives forever as our High Priest at the right hand of God. Please note it is one thing to confess with your mouth, which is necessary, and another thing to let your actions and character affirm your confession. If you are in Christ, then you are in a covenant relationship with God the Father through the man Jesus Christ. He is our advocate and mediator between us and God.

What is this covenant, and how can we be sure that we are keeping the covenant? According to Webster's Dictionary, a covenant is a **written agreement or promise** usually **under seal between two or more parties,** especially **for the performance of some action.** It's important to pay attention to the key elements of this definition.

When we received Jesus Christ and made our open confession that He is our Lord and Savior, we entered this covenant relationship with God. We enter an agreement that Jesus is Lord over our lives and that God promised to pardon all our sins. Our public confession and baptism are our sealing of the agreement, while the Father's gift of His Holy Spirit is His seal upon us that we are His, He in us, and we in Him.

Consider the following scripture. "By this we know that we abide in Him, and He in us, because He has given us of His Spirit. Whoever confesses that Jesus is the Son of God, God abides in him, and he in God" (1 John 4:13, 15 NKJV). The parties of this covenant are all the saints individually and collectively: the Father, the Son, and the Holy Spirit. The required action for us to perform is to abide in Him by keeping His Word or commandments.

Even before we entered this agreement, the Father, through Jesus Christ, already performed the most important act by the suffering, death, and resurrection of His Son. For reference, please read and consider the following scriptures: John 14: 23–24; Romans 5:8; and John 15:10–17. There are many more scriptures, but these are a good starting point.

Now that we understand the meaning of covenant, let's look at the written covenant, which I like to call the covenant of peace. This is what the scriptures records concerning Jesus and the new covenant in Hebrews 8:6–12. Also, please note that the old covenant was instituted under Moses with all the Mosaic laws. The new covenant with Jesus Christ as Mediator and High Priest makes the first covenant obsolete.

But now He has obtained a more excellent ministry, inasmuch as He is also Mediator of a better covenant, which was established on better promises. For if that first covenant had been faultless, then no place would have been sought for a second. Because finding fault with them, He says: "Behold, the days are coming, says the Lord, when I will make a new covenant with the house of Israel and with the house of Judah—not according to the covenant that I made with their fathers in the day when I took them by the hand to lead them out of the land of Egypt; because they did not continue in My covenant, and I disregarded them, says the Lord. For this is the covenant that I will make with the house of Israel after those days, says the Lord: I will put My laws in their mind and write them on their hearts; and I will be their God, and they shall be My people. None of them shall teach his neighbor, and none his brother, saying, 'Know the Lord,' for all shall know Me, from the least of them to the greatest of them. For I will be merciful to their unrighteousness, and their sins and their lawless deeds I will remember no more" (Hebrews 8:6–12 NKJV).

What makes this covenant unique is, firstly, the fact that we have an eternal High Priest, Jesus Christ, who forever lives to intercede on our behalf. Under the old covenant, the high priest first had to offer a sacrifice for his own sins before going into the presence of God on our behalf. Under this new covenant, Jesus abides eternally at the right hand of the Father and is therefore able to continually make intercessions on our behalf.

Secondly, He put His laws into our minds and wrote them in our hearts. This is why we are called to renew our minds and study to show ourselves approved by God.

When we meditate on His Word and live by the living Word of God, we come into agreement with His Word abiding in our heart and mind. The Holy Spirit within us then inscribes God's Word into our heart. As the scripture says, "I will give you a new heart and put a new spirit within you; I will take the heart of stone out of your flesh and give you a heart of flesh" (Ezek. 36:26 NKJV).

Thirdly, He will be our God, and we will be His people. What made this so difficult under the first covenant was the constant presence of sin. But now as we fellowship with Him, there is a constant cleansing of our sins so He can dwell within our hearts (See 1 John 1:7 & 2 Cor. 6:17–18). This does not give us licenses to break the covenant by practicing sinning, but if we do sin, our High Priest makes intercession for us, and the covenant remains intact.

Fourthly, we all know Him, and we know that we know Him because we keep His commandments, and He has given us His Spirit. "Now by this we know that we know Him, if we keep His commandments" (1 John 2:3 NKJV).

Although we may not be perfect at keeping Father's commandments, this covenant does not depend on our own efforts. This covenant rests entirely on the finished work of Jesus Christ, who perfectly kept all the commandments. Because this covenant has nothing to do with our own works, it is entirely a free gift of God's grace to all. Lastly, because of the finished work of Christ, Father is merciful regarding our unrighteousness, sins, and lawless deeds, and He will not bring our deeds into His remembrance. When Father looks at us, He sees the covering of Christ, the righteousness of Christ. These five points illustrates the uniqueness of God's covenant and grace toward us.

Jesus Christ Our Advocate & High Priest

You have the right to proper counsel, Advocate, mediator, and the High Priest to pray for you. It is always best to have a lawyer and a pastor ready and available to you before you get into trouble. Glory be to God, and thank You, Jesus, for always being there and available when we call.

When was the last time you had an unrighteousness thought, lusted, lied, took something that didn't belong to you, coveted something someone else had, or maybe just took out your self-righteous anger on someone? The point is that we all sin and so we all need the sinless High Priest to intercede on our behalf. Here is what the scriptures say, "As it is written: 'There is none righteous, no, not one; There is none who understands; There is none who seeks after God. They have all turned aside; They have together become unprofitable; There is none who does good, no, not one'" (Rom. 3:10–12 NKJV).

God already knows we will sin, even those who are in Christ Jesus. He has also made provisions for our sinful actions but also given us power to not practice sinning. We can read in the scriptures where the apostle John said, "If we say that we have no sin, we deceive ourselves, and the truth is not in us. If we confess our sins, He is faithful and just to forgive us our sins and to cleanse us from all unrighteousness" (1 John 1:8–9 NKJV). John goes on to say, "My little children, these things I write to you, so that you may not sin. And if anyone sins, we have an Advocate with the Father, Jesus Christ the righteous. And He Himself is the propitiation for our sins, and not for ours only but also for the whole world" (1 John 2:1–2 NKJV).

Although we can overcome sin and temptation, within our flesh, evil is present, and its desire is to be sinful. Until our fleshly bodies are transformed, we will always be capable of sinning, and we have accusers who point their finger at us in order to bring charges against us and God. This is why we have and need our Advocate Jesus Christ, who not only advocates on our behalf but as High Priest, He also prays for us. Jesus has given us all things that pertains to life and godliness to guarantee our successful transformation. This is why we are called upon to renew our minds and be transformed. Through the knowledge and promises of God, we can live in His divine nature and overcome the sinful desires of our flesh.

We have a High Priest who can sympathize with our weakness because he was also tempted as we are, yet without sinning.

Having overcome all, including death, Jesus Christ now lives forever as our permanent High Priest, making intercession for us. When we sin, Jesus is the only one Who can advocate on our behalf. No one else can go directly to the Father concerning sins, but we have direct access to the Father. The scriptures say, "there is one God, and there is one mediator between God and men, the man Christ Jesus" (1 Tim. 2:5 ESV).

Whenever we sin, we are breaking the covenant and must have legal counsel capable of standing before God on our behalf. Jesus, being fully man and having all the fullness of the Godhead, makes Him the perfect and only Mediator, Advocate, and High Priest between us and God. I have had the pleasure of witnessing Christ as Mediator and Advocate.

On January 6, 2022, at approximately 9:30 p.m., I was praying, and the Holy Spirit was praying through me. At first, I was in the kitchen with my wife and had this overwhelming need to go and pray. So, I ran into the bedroom and knelt down by my bed to pray. The Holy Spirit began to pray through me in tongues. When the Spirit stopped praying, I saw, as though watching a video, the Spirit shifted from me and spoke to Christ the Son. He was seated at the right of what seemed like a judge's bench in a courtroom, and the Father was seated as the judge. As The Holy Spirit spoke to Christ on my behalf, I then saw the Lord stand up and speak to Father on my behalf. The Father looked at me and said to me, "**A judgment has been made in your favor!**" I then asked, "Why must there be a judgment in my favor?" In other words, what is going on, and what's about to happen? He answered, "Treachery!" This vision was an answer to the Holy Spirit and my prayers concerning my student loans, although I am still not certain what was meant by treachery.

On October 4, 2021, President Biden passed a temporary law by which potentially all my student loans could be forgiven. I had accumulated more than 150 thousand dollars in student loans, some of which stretched back to the 1990s. However, because I had consolidated my loans, I was not qualified for other forgiveness programs. In 2015, I hired a lawyer to file the paperwork for me to be in the right repayment plan for the ten-year forgiveness program for public employees. But I found out in 2019 that I was not in the right payment plan and had to start over. This adjusted my time in the repayment plan to conclude in the year 2029. This also meant that I would not be able to retire before this time. So, I applied for the forgiveness program under the new law President Biden passed. But after I applied for this new forgiveness plan, I was denied and was told that I would have to remain in a ten-year program, which would conclude sometime in the years 2028 or 2029. So, after all these years of trying to pay off my student loans, I had to start all over again. I was really hoping to qualify for this temporary program that President Biden passed. Needless to say, this was heartbreaking being denied, but I kept praying.

My prayer was answered at 7:30 a.m. on Tuesday, January 11, 2022, five days after the Holy Spirit prayed for me and I saw the vision. After arriving at work that Tuesday morning, I called and was talking to my wife as usual. **Then, I received an email saying that a decision was made in my favor.** It was from the student loan PEN loans. So, I opened the app on my phone to check my account. The app said I couldn't access my account; this app was only for people who had a loan balance. My heart leaped, and tears began to flow down my face. So, I somewhat gathered myself and went to the website to check. All my loans reported a ZERO balance. By this time, I was crying out loud and praising God at the same time. I called back my wife and told her, then printed out the paperwork.

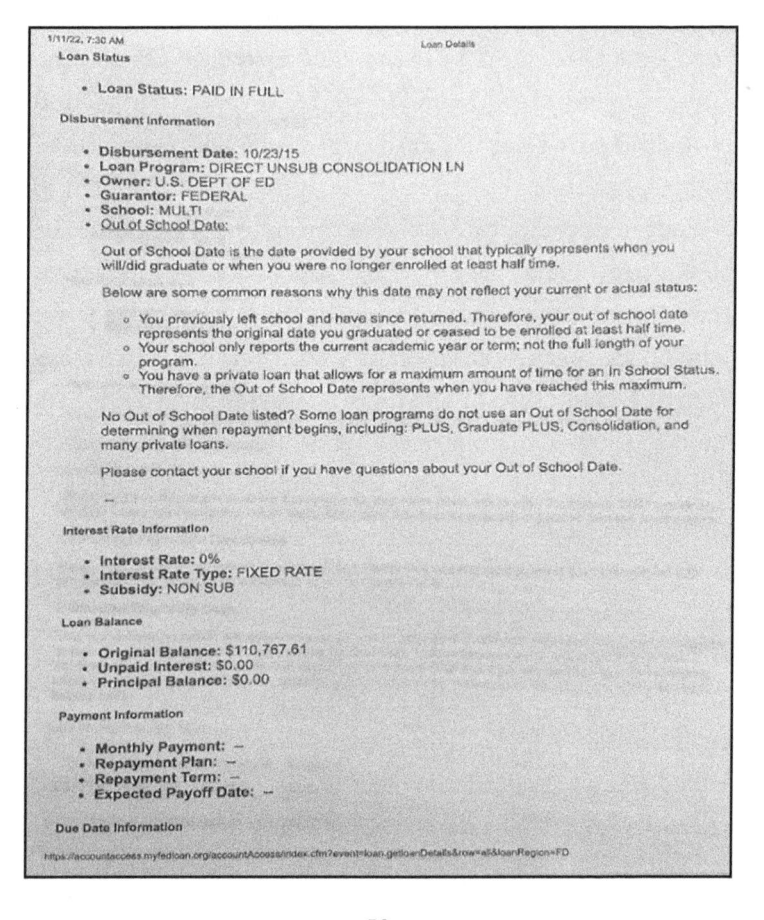

1/11/22, 7:30 AM — Loan Details

Loan Status

- **Loan Status:** PAID IN FULL

Disbursement Information

- **Disbursement Date:** 10/23/15
- **Loan Program:** DIRECT UNSUB CONSOLIDATION LN
- **Owner:** U.S. DEPT OF ED
- **Guarantor:** FEDERAL
- **School:** MULTI
- **Out of School Date:**

Out of School Date is the date provided by your school that typically represents when you will/did graduate or when you were no longer enrolled at least half time.

Below are some common reasons why this date may not reflect your current or actual status:

- You previously left school and have since returned. Therefore, your out of school date represents the original date you graduated or ceased to be enrolled at least half time.
- Your school only reports the current academic year or term; not the full length of your program.
- You have a private loan that allows for a maximum amount of time for an In School Status. Therefore, the Out of School Date represents when you have reached this maximum.

No Out of School Date listed? Some loan programs do not use an Out of School Date for determining when repayment begins, including: PLUS, Graduate PLUS, Consolidation, and many private loans.

Please contact your school if you have questions about your Out of School Date.

Interest Rate Information

- **Interest Rate:** 0%
- **Interest Rate Type:** FIXED RATE
- **Subsidy:** NON SUB

Loan Balance

- **Original Balance:** $110,767.61
- **Unpaid Interest:** $0.00
- **Principal Balance:** $0.00

Payment Information

- **Monthly Payment:** --
- **Repayment Plan:** --
- **Repayment Term:** --
- **Expected Payoff Date:** --

Due Date Information

https://accountaccess.myfedloan.org/accountAccess/index.cfm?event=loan.getloanDetails&row=all&loanRegion=FD

This is just one of my loans. The Holy Spirit prayed, Christ Advocated, and Father made a judgment on my behalf. Glory hallelujah to God my Father, to Jesus Christ my Lord, and Holy Spirit, my helper and comforter.

Access to the Father
(the Only Sovereign God)

He is the one and only Sovereign God, and we can communicate with Him! Wow! The scripture records, "If you then, being evil, know how to give good gifts to your children, how much more will your Father who is in heaven give good things to those who ask Him!" (Matt. 7:11 NKJV).

This is a very profound statement made by Jesus Christ in speaking to a crowd of people. It is not merely the fact that we are evil and the Father is good. Nor is it just that the Good Father gives good things to those who ask Him. Below the surface here is the comparison of fatherhood and, most importantly, our relationship with the Good Father. Jesus plainly stated that God is our Good Father and that we can ask Him directly concerning all our cares. He did not say that we must go through some ritualistic exercise or that we must ask Him to ask the Father for us. He said, "how much more will your Father who is in heaven give good things to those who ask Him?" Furthermore, the scriptures also record that Jesus also said, "In that day you will ask in My name, and I am not saying to you that I will ask the Father on your behalf [because it will be unnecessary]; for the Father Himself [tenderly] loves you, because you have loved Me and have believed that I came from the Father. I came from the Father and have come into the world; again, I am leaving the world and going to the Father" (John 16:26–28 AMP). Because we love Jesus and believe that He came from the Father, we have been given this great privilege of having access to the Father.

Because Jesus the Son of God has returned to the Father, we now can, in Jesus's name, ask Father directly. The Father loves us, and the veil of separation has been removed, granting us direct access to the Father into the most holy place. When we say we accept Jesus into our hearts, that is, into our bodily temple, it is not just Jesus Who enters. He doesn't travel alone! "Jesus answered and said to him, 'If anyone loves Me, he will keep My word; and My Father will love him, and We will come to him and make Our home with him" (John 14:23 NKJV). "At that day you will know that I am in My Father, and you in Me, and I in you" (John 14:20 NKJV).

When Jesus returned to the Father, He was glorified with the same glory that He had with the Father before He was incarnated on earth. He and the Father are one; when Christ enters our bodily temple, so does the Father. Also, for that matter, so does the Holy Spirit. If you have been baptized by Jesus with the Holy Spirit, then you have the Father, Son, and Holy Spirit living within you. Remember what the first commandment says, "Hear, O Israel: The Lord our God, the Lord is one!" (Deut. 6:4 NKJV).

I was reminded of this privilege in a dream I had on Thursday morning of August 24, 2023. I was battling with the enemy and had apparently forgotten or didn't know that I had free access to my heavenly Father. The enemy was coming at me, and Christ was standing in one corner, and Holy Spirit said to me, "You have access to go directly to the Father." So, I turned around and ran to rest in Father's arms. As I had turned to go to my Father, a dark spirit entered my bedroom. I felt it get on the bed, and the shadow of it came down at me as I quickly moved to embrace Father, then I woke up.

Thank You, Father, that You are stronger than all. You have me in the palms of Your hands, and no one or no demon can pluck me away from Your hands. Thank You, Father, for the right, through Christ Jesus, of access to You. Thank You that I can come directly to You, Father, and rest in Your arms. Amen!

My children have a right to approach me, commune with me, and access any good treasures that are mine. Even when I don't have, I will find a way to give to and help my children. How much more will our heavenly Father give to us when we ask Him? How much more does He desire to communicate and fellowship with us? This is why Jesus is called Immanuel, meaning God with us, not just around some place but in us and present with us. It has always been Father's will to dwell with us and for us to be in constant fellowship with Him. Therefore, we must learn to submit to the Spirit and allow Him to draw us into the presence of the Father. We must learn to be present in the moment with Him.

Have you ever been someplace with someone who is just not present, in the moment, with you? We can start by acknowledging the fact that we have a right of access to be present with our heavenly Father at this moment and always.

Your Teacher, Counselor, & Seal of Approval (Holy Spirit)

In our quest to understand the Trinity of God, we sometimes humanize God and begin to categorize Him. There are some things we do not fully understand and certainly cannot humanly explain, but these things must be discerned by faith. However, we must all remember that we are the created, and He is the Creator. The only way to comprehend God in human terms is Jesus Christ! He is the expressed image of God in human form. By faith, we must accept the truth that God is One, yet in three distinct ways. The Holy Spirit Whom we often refer to as the third person in the Godhead is One with Father and Son. He proceeds from the Father and is also called the Spirit of Truth. He comes to us directly from Father to forever be with us and for very specific reasons.

> *"If you love Me, keep My commandments. And I will pray the Father, and He will give you another Helper, that He may abide with you forever—the Spirit of truth, whom the world cannot receive, because it neither sees Him nor knows Him; but you know Him, for He dwells with you and will be in you"* (John 14:15–17 NKJV).

Firstly, the Holy Spirit is given to us as an Advocate, a Counselor, or a Helper. He is a constant companion on our sojourn in this world. His work is never done! He works tirelessly to keep us safe in Christ. Though we have grieved Him, despite our wavering and even through our doubts and all our struggles, He remains faithfully devoted to our eternal salvation. As our advocate and counselor, the Spirit of God is our constant companion and guide to help us in the way.

If you made an inquiry about most wealthy people, you would find that they have a lawyer on retainer. Most of them seek advice or counsel from their lawyer before they make any significant decisions. When we received Christ as Lord and Savior, we became a member of the royal family of God. Therefore, Father provided for all of us, His children, the Holy Spirit as our Counselor, Advocate, and Helper for every step of our journey. The problem is that most of us are still living like paupers rather than royals. Therefore, we do what we're used to doing. We maintain the "status quo" rather than availing ourselves of the power, counsel, and glory given to us as children of God. Furthermore, we are ambassadors for Christ, and what ambassador makes haphazard decisions rather than consult with legal counsel and the government they represent?

We must learn to communicate with our Counselor and follow His guidance in everything we do. The Holy Spirit, our Counselor, dwells within us and will abide with us forever. Therefore, we are never alone and never without His counsel. We are workers together with Him and must learn to trust Him, pray with Him, communicate with Him, and maintain a constant fellowship with Him. As ambassadors, we bear witness of Christ, and the Holy Spirit also bears witness of Christ. Together, we bear witness to the world of the truth of the gospel of Jesus Christ. "But when the Helper comes, whom I will send to you from the Father, the Spirit of Truth, who proceeds from the Father, he will bear witness about me. And you also will bear witness, because you have been with me from the beginning" (John 15:26–27 ESV).

Secondly, The Spirit of Truth is our teacher Who reminds us of all lessons learned. "But the Helper, the Holy Spirit, whom the Father will send in My name, He will teach you all things, and bring to your remembrance all things that I said to you" (John 14:26 NKJV). This is significant because the Word of God is more than just words on a page. The revealing of Jesus Christ through the Word of God is a function of the Holy Spirit.

The Spirit of Truth opens our understanding and quickens us, giving us an insight beyond the mere words on the pages. Even after reading the Word and not fully understanding what we have read, the Holy Spirit brings it back to our minds, teaching us as we go through our days. He often uses people, nature, or even just speaking to us, Spirit to spirit, unfolding and downloading wisdom and principles we have never even thought about before.

This is what Father declares to us in His covenant with us, saying, "I will put My laws in their mind and write them on their hearts; and I will be their God, and they shall be My people. None of them shall teach his neighbor, and none his brother, saying, 'Know the Lord,' for all shall know Me, from the least of them to the greatest of them" (Jer. 31:33–34 NKJV). Jesus also said, "They shall all be taught by God" (John 6:45 NKJV). We should not find it strange that the Holy Spirit speaks to us and wants to teach us all things.

Thirdly, Holy Spirit is as a seal or mark upon every child of God, designating that we belong to God our Father and Jesus Christ our Lord. Since God is Spirit and not flesh nor blood, the only way for us to have His "DNA," fleshly speaking, is for us to have His Spirit within us. The scriptures tell us that God has given to us His Spirit so that we can call Him Abba Father. It tells us that the Spirit Himself testifies, in other words, attests, that we are children of God and therefore joint heirs with Christ.

Therefore, if the Holy Spirit is abiding in you, you can be certain that you are a child of God. When the first believing Gentiles show their faith in Jesus Christ, the Father bore witness that they belong to Him by giving them the Holy Spirit. The Father showed the apostles that these Gentiles, though uncircumcised in their flesh, their faith was pleasing to Him. The Father's testimony and speaking action was to pour out His Spirit upon them. It is therefore clear that a proof that one is an accepted child of God is the Presence of the Holy Spirit in them. The gift of the Holy Spirit is like Christ putting a ring on your finger as a seal of His love and intent to marry. Consider the following scriptures!

"And God, who knows the heart, bore witness to them, by giving them the Holy Spirit just as he did to us" (Acts 15:8 ESV).

"For you did not receive the spirit of bondage again to fear, but you received the Spirit of adoption by whom we cry out, "Abba, Father." The Spirit Himself bears witness with our spirit that we are children of God, and if children, then heirs—heirs of God and joint heirs with Christ, if indeed we suffer with Him, that we may also be glorified together" (Rom. 8:15–17 NKJV).

"By this we know that we abide in Him, and He in us, because He has given us of His Spirit" (1 John 4:13 NKJV).

"Now He who establishes us with you in Christ and has anointed us is God, who also has sealed us and given us the Spirit in our hearts as a guarantee" (2 Cor. 1:21–22 NKJV).

Your Right to Remain Silent: Be Still and Know

Sometimes we get into trouble, and we don't behave like royal children of God. Growing up on the island of Jamaica, I was always gone someplace with my friends. Most of the time, we were somewhere doing something we knew we weren't supposed to be doing. But that's what children often do. They throw tantrums and are often trying to do the things that they are told not to do. The unique nature of parenthood is that even when children fall because of disobedience, the parents are willingly there to lift and pick them up, helping them get back on track.

My wife pointed out a scripture to me in John 15:2. In this chapter of the Bible, Jesus is speaking about abiding in Him. In this scripture, Jesus is talking about a vine in Him that is not being fruitful at the moment. So, what does the loving Father do? He lifts the vine, picks it up off the ground, and lifts it up to a place where it can now become fruitful. Yes, some translations says that He takes away that branch, but the same Greek word (Airo) used is also translated to lift-up. (G142 Strongs Concordance)

Can you remember a time in your life when you fell, messed up, or were in some difficulty and your parents were there to help you to get back up on your feet? The scripture says that if we, being evil, know how to do good for our children, how much more will the Good Father do good for us. Father is not about slaying the wounded; He desires Mercy and not sacrifice. He is long-suffering, not willing that anyone should perish but that all may come to repentance (2 Pet. 3:9). Therefore, though we fall time and time again, He is patient with us, helping us to get back on track.

Sometimes children may get into legal trouble and sometimes enemies may try to harm them. Enemies may be anyone or thing that wants to harm a child or people for various reasons. But sometimes we do get into legal trouble, or we break the covenant and get into spiritual trouble. Now, especially in the Black community, our children are taught that they have the right to remain silent. Indeed, if you are ever a target of the police or any investigation, this is a right you may want to exercise.

How does this work in the kingdom of God, in the spiritual realm? We were told about, and sometimes we talk about the weapons of our warfare, but I don't recall the right to remain silent being one of them. Well, one of those weapons is the right to remain silent and be still. I am very guilty of not using this weapon because I instinctively want to come to my own defense or just feel like I must do something about a situation.

Jesus is our primary example to follow. To be clear, Jesus did no wrongdoing and was indeed sinless and innocent. However, we can draw from his example where he fought against the powers of darkness working through the authorities of that time. At the most sorrowful point of His life after praying for Father's will to be done, Jesus exercised His right to remain silent. After being arrested by the Jewish temple police and while in the custody of the Roman police, He rarely spoke a word. He completely entrusted the events of His life and eventually His death into the sovereign will of His Father. He did not complain or tried to talk His way out of His situation.

Once He prayed for His Father's will to be done, He left His case at the altar. Consider this prophetic scripture about this particular time in the life of Jesus Christ. "He was oppressed, and He was afflicted, Yet He opened not His mouth; He was led as a lamb to the slaughter, and as a sheep before its shearers is silent, So He opened not His mouth" (Isa. 53:7 NKJV). Most times people associate silence with weakness, but it is often the opposite. His silence was a showing of His complete trust in the sovereignty of God.

This is affirmed also by the way He answered Pontius Pilate, which was one of the few times that He spoke. Jesus answered Pilate, "You could have no power at all against Me unless it had been given you from above" (John 19:11a NKJV). This is a profound attestation of the faith of Jesus in the sovereignty of God. It is also a lesson that we would do well to learn from. When we know that we have heard from God, we can confidently go forward even in the face of great challenges, knowing that Father's Sovereignty will prevail.

We see also in the days of Daniel, the Babylonian king made a decree that men ought not to pray for thirty days to any god but must make petitions to him only. Anyone who prayed to God would be thrown into the lion's den full of hungry lions. But Daniel continued his customary prayer practices, praying to God three times daily. There's no record of Daniel complaining, defending himself, nor anything like that. He had already prayed, so he remained silent. The only time he spoke concerning this situation was after being delivered by God and the king came to remove him from the lion's den. Sometimes, after praying to God, we must exercise our right to be silent and trust the sovereignty of God. These moments are when we must be still and let God work on our behalf. In Psalm 46:10, the scripture tells us to be still and know that He is God.

God's Divine Covering

We can truly learn to be still even in the midst of the stormy circumstances of our lives. This is because of the assurance that God's divine covering is a hedge of protection, blessings, and grace around those who fears Him and turn from evil. The book of Job predates almost all the other books of the Bible. So, before we read about Abraham and Moses and all the patriarchs of the Bible, we can read the book of Job and see how God dealt with those who reverenced Him. Long before there were any laws or covenants formed, Father's divine covering was available to those who feared him and departed from evil.

It is important to understand this divine covering, with which God covered Job. God placed an edge of protection around Job so that no evil would befall him. This covering was because Job was found to be blameless and upright before God. It is also important to understand this story of Job's life and experiences because it shows us the sovereignty of God, our relationship to God, and the legal positioning of Satan. Many in the church today will have us believe that Satan still presents himself before God and accuses us to God. I believe that this is an incorrect teaching, and although it had its place in the past, it's no longer the case.

So, in the book of Job, we see the sons of God gathering at appointed times to present themselves before God. The scripture then goes on to say that Satan also came to present himself. But why was he allowed in the presence of God in the first place? Why did he even bother to go and present himself? I believe the answer to these questions lies in the authority that Satan stole by deceiving mankind. Satan's ability to go before God showed that there are laws within the kingdom of God that must be followed and that God honors His kingdom laws. If we examine the scripture in Job 2:1, we will read a second time how the sons of God came to present themselves, and Satan also came to present himself before the Lord. This was a customary gathering or reporting to God by those who held authority in the kingdom of God. Please note that Satan was stripped of all authority he had, and Jesus the Christ now holds all authority in heaven and earth under the Father.

> *"Again, there was a day when the sons of God came to present themselves before the Lord, and Satan also came among them to present himself before the Lord"* (Job 2:1 ESV).

If we imagine for a moment a vast kingdom having many territories, it will only seem practical to have individuals in charge of the different territories. Consider also that the Bible declares that Jesus is the king of kings meaning that there are kings underneath him who are subject to him. Also consider that every king has a kingdom over which he or she rules. The earthly realm was given to mankind to rule over and have dominion. By means of deception, authority over this earthly realm, was turned over to Satan. It is because of this authority, which he possessed, past tense, why he was allowed to go and present himself before God, the sovereign ruler over all. Although the Bible is not clear as to what occurred with Satan prior to the creation of mankind, we know that he was cast out of Heaven away from the presence of God. We can read in the book of Isaiah, where iniquity was found in his heart, and he was cast out of heaven into the pit.

> *"You said in your heart, 'I will ascend to heaven; above the stars of God, I will set my throne on high; I will sit on the mount of assembly in the far reaches of the north; I will ascend above the heights of the clouds; I will make myself like the Most High.' But you are brought down to Sheol, to the far reaches of the pit"* (Isa. 14:13–15 ESV).

We see that Satan had already lost access to the presence of God. So, why then, do we read in Job that he is presenting himself before God. It is because he deceived and stole this authority from mankind. And so, we can read in the book of Job and see Satan boasting in his pride, how he walks on the earth, "to and fro." Yet because of the divine covering of God over Job, the devil could do nothing to him and only watch from a distance as God prospered Job and protected everyone under Job's rule. Consider the following scripture.

> *The Lord said to Satan, "From where have you come?" Satan answered the Lord and said, "From going to and fro on the earth, and from walking up and down on it." And the Lord said to Satan, "Have you considered my servant Job, that there is none like him on the earth, a blameless and upright man, who fears God and turns away from evil?" Then Satan answered the Lord and said, "Does Job fear God for no reason? Have you not put a hedge around him and his house and all that he has on every side? You have blessed the work of his hands, and his possessions have increased in the land"* (Job 1:7–10 ESV).

When considering this Scripture, we must ask ourselves a few questions; rather, we must ask of the scripture a few questions. The first question we should ask is, why is the Lord asking Satan, "From where have you come"? The Lord God is omniscient and therefore did not need to inquire from Satan, "From where have you come"? I believe His question was a means of Him saying to Satan, "you are here only because of stolen authority." To which Satan responded, "Yeah, I'm not in the pit. I'm walking to and fro, back and forth, and up and down the earth." This is just my interpretation of their conversation. Then God responded to him, "I have a blameless and upright manservant in the earth who fears God and turns away from evil." So, Satan incited God to remove his divine covering from his servant Job. However, note that not only did Satan need permission to do anything to Job, but he also had to be subject to the limitations set by the sovereign God. And this tells us that there is no authority or power in this world that does not come from God.

We can see this also in the situation with Jesus standing before Pontius Pilate. Jesus told him that he would have no power over him unless it was given to him from above. Therefore, we can be patient in our sufferings, knowing that God is not only in full control, but he also sees all things, knows all things, and cares about us. Note also, that the goal of Satan was not only to get Job to curse God but also to get him to charge God with wrongdoing.

The goal of Satan remains the same today; he's trying to get us to bring a false charge against God and walk in rebellion to God's authority. This is a part of the reason why we hear people falsely declare all the time, "If there's a God, why do certain things happen." It is an act of pointing the finger at God and saying, "How could you let this happen?" However, after Satan had stripped Job of all his earthly possessions, Job still did not sin against God nor charge God with wrongdoing. Job's response was to worship God and to humble himself before God.

> *"Then Job arose and tore his robe and shaved his head and fell on the ground and worshiped. And he said, 'Naked I came from my mother's womb, and naked shall I return. The Lord gave, and the Lord has taken away; blessed be the name of the*

Lord.' In all this Job did not sin or charge God with wrong" (Job 1:20–22 ESV).

There is so much more to be learned from Job's experience. We can see that even in the midst of all that the enemy tried to do to him, God's divine covering was still over Job. Therefore, Satan had to be obedient to God's limitations as to what he was allowed to do to Job. It is also important to observe that one of the devices of Satan is to get us to accuse God. So not only is he the accuser of the brethren, but he also wants God's people to accuse God.

What is most important to understand concerning Satan's authority is that he no longer has any authority to go before God, nor can he go to heaven to present himself in anyway. His legal authority was revoked when Christ won the victory over sin, death, hell, and the grave. Jesus the Christ made an open spectacle of Satan. The man Jesus took back all the authority that Satan had deceptively stolen from mankind. And now Jesus the Christ is seated at the right hand of power of the sovereign God, and He forever lives to make intercession for us.

Jesus said, "All authority has been given to Me in heaven and on earth" (Matt. 28:18 NKJV). I believe this is why the apostle Paul, in the book of Romans, declared, "Who shall bring a charge against God's elect . . . Who is to condemn?" (Rom. 8:33–34). Well, you might say what about Satan. Jesus said, "I saw Satan fall like lightning from heaven" (Luke 10:18 NKJV). If we consider the following scriptures, it is clear that when the rule of Christ was in place, Satan was cast down to the earth, and therefore no longer has any authority in the presence of God.

> *She gave birth to a male child, one who is to rule all the nations with a rod of iron, but **her child was caught up to God and to his throne** . . . **Now war arose in heaven, Michael and his angels fighting against the dragon. And the dragon and his angels fought back, but he was defeated, and there was no longer any place for them in heaven. And the great dragon was thrown down, that ancient serpent, who is called the devil and Satan, the deceiver of the whole world—he was thrown down to the earth, and his angels were thrown down with him.** And I heard a loud voice in heaven, saying, "**Now the salvation and the power and the kingdom of our God and the authority of his Christ have come**, for the accuser of our brothers has been thrown down, who accuses them day and night before our God"* (Rev. 12:5, 7–10 ESV, emphasis added).

> *"Therefore, rejoice, O heavens and you who dwell in them! But woe to you, O earth and sea, for the devil has come down to you in great wrath, because he knows that his time is short!"* (Rev. 12:12 ESV).

The woman who gave birth to the child is a reference to the nation of Israel, the Christ being born from the lineage of David, tribe of Judah. Jesus the Christ is also the only one who has ascended into heaven and is seated at the right hand of power on his throne, where he rules forevermore. So, although Satan and his angels fought against it, they were defeated. Now Christ has all authority, and Satan has been cast down to the earth. This is an event that has already occurred and not something waiting to happen in the future.

If while Satan had authority, he still had to get permission from God do anything to God's servants, how much less can he do now that he no longer holds any authority? I believe this is why the apostle Paul says,

> *Who shall separate us from the love of Christ? Shall tribulation, or distress, or persecution, or famine, or nakedness, or danger, or sword? For **I am sure that neither death nor life, nor angels nor rulers, nor things present nor things to come, nor powers, nor height nor depth, nor anything else in all creation, will be able to separate us from the love of God in Christ Jesus our Lord*** (Rom. 8:35, 38–39 ESV, emphasis added).

God has us covered even though we experience sufferings! Sufferings are a necessary part of our transformation as we learn to resist the devil and submit ourselves to God. Like Job, we are expected to humble ourselves under the mighty hand of God and respond with thanksgivings and true worship. So, when the apostles endured sufferings, they responded with thanksgivings and worship that they were counted worthy to suffer for the cause of Christ.

There is another side to our fellowship with Christ that is rarely spoken of; it's called the fellowship of His suffering. Furthermore, the scriptures also say that if we suffer with Him, then we shall reign with Him. Consider what the apostle Paul says, "that I may know Him and the power of His resurrection, and the fellowship of His sufferings, being conformed to His death" (Phil. 3:10 NKJV).

The Defeated Accuser

There is another point of view to consider in response to anyone who may think Satan has any right to accuse a believer before God. Why do the scriptures, which cannot be broken, says there is NOW no more condemnation for those who are in Christ Jesus? Let us consider these scriptures carefully!

> *"Therefore, there is now no condemnation [no guilty verdict, no punishment] for those who are in Christ Jesus [who believe in Him as personal Lord and Savior]"* (Rom. 8:1 AMP)

> *"He who believes in Him is not condemned; but he who does not believe is condemned already,*

because he has not believed in the name of the only begotten Son of God" (John 3:18 NKJV).

The scriptures clearly tell us that now being in Christ and clothed with His righteousness, we are not under any condemnation. Christ knows everything there is to know about our past, present, and future. He has redeemed, purchased, us while we were still in our sinful condition. He then cleaned us up and justified us. If He does not bring a charge against us, then no one else has any right to bring a charge against us. Please consider that any accuser must have grounds in the court of law in order to bring a charge against someone. He must also have a legal interest or rights to protect or seek remedy, that is, recompense, for a wrong done against him. At other times, the state may bring a charge against someone for wrongs or crimes against the state.

The Accuser, Satan, no longer has any standing in the courts of heaven. Jesus the Redeemer paid the remedy or compensation for us. We are His purchased possessions. When He said, "It is finished," on the cross, (Joh.19:30) He also took care of all our sin issue. Please remember that we are in Him and clothed in His righteousness. Our lives are hidden in Him, and the life we now live we live unto God through Him. Furthermore, Jesus says that we are not of this world but are ambassadors, representing His kingdom in this world.

As ambassadors, we are under a different governing authority and therefore are immune from prosecution by the kingdom of this world. As I explained before, Satan has no authority in the courtroom of heaven. Therefore, God Himself rebuked Satan because of Christ and clothed us in His righteousness. Satan was thrown out of the courts of the LORD because he had no case concerning God's chosen people. I want us to consider the scriptures of Joshua the high priest in Zechariah 3.

> *Then the guiding angel showed me Joshua the high priest [representing disobedient, sinful Israel] standing before the Angel of the Lord, and Satan standing at Joshua's right hand to be his adversary and to accuse him. And the Lord said to Satan, "The Lord rebuke you, Satan! Even the Lord, who [now and ever] has chosen Jerusalem, rebuke you! Is this not a log snatched and rescued from the fire?"* (Zech. 3:1-2 AMP)

Here we find an angel of the LORD revealing to Zechariah what is to come as concerning the people of God. Joshua the high priest stands as a representation of the sinful people whom the LORD has chosen to save. The function of the high priest is to stand in proxy for all the people who he represents and for himself. In this case, the priest can be viewed as the man Jesus, who is also called Joshua. Joshua means "Jehovah saved." (Strongs Concordance) Note that he is the high priest of those being saved. Joshua is standing before the Angel of the LORD Who represents Christ here. Please note that Jesus the Christ is both 100 percent man capable of sinning but did not sin, and He is also 100 percent the Son of God, incapable of sinning, Who rules over all the LORD's house and courts.

Satan the accuser is standing by the right hand of Joshua to accuse him of sin. The accuser, Satan, is therefore accusing all the LORD's chosen people of sins. Please note that Satan is standing by the right hand of Joshua, which means Satan has the authority to make the accusations. As I explained before, this authority he had stolen through deception from the first Adam. But now that the second Adam, Jesus Christ, has been given all authority, Satan no longer has this right.

But here we see the LORD, the Self-Existing One; God Himself rebukes Satan to save the LORD's chosen people. Note that the LORD did not say Joshua is innocent but rather declared that these chosen people have been rescued from the fire, the sentence of condemnation. Satan is silent before the Sovereign LORD. Please note that after the LORD rebukes Satan the accuser, Satan is no longer mentioned. The accuser lost his case, and the accused, although guilty of sin, is given grace, full pardon, rescued from the fire, and clothed in righteousness. Let's ponder the next set of verses.

> *Now Joshua was clothed with filthy (nauseatingly vile) garments and was standing before the Angel [of the Lord]. He spoke to those who stood before Him, saying, "Remove the filthy garments from him." And He said to Joshua, "See, I have caused your wickedness to be taken away from you, and I will clothe and beautify you with rich robes [of*

forgiveness]." And I (Zechariah) said, "Let them put a clean turban on his head." So, they put a clean turban on his head and clothed him with [rich] garments. And the Angel of the Lord stood by. And the Angel of the Lord [solemnly and earnestly] admonished Joshua, saying, "Thus says the Lord of hosts, 'If you will walk in My ways [that is, remain faithful] and perform My service, then you will also govern My house and have charge of My courts, and I will give you free access [to My presence] among these who are standing here'" (Zech. 3:3–7 AMP).

Why is Joshua clothed in filthy garments if he represents Jesus who never sinned? Although Jesus or Joshua the high priest never sinned, he became sin for us. He took upon himself all our sins. So, the man Jesus became sinful on our account, but the Angel of the LORD, Christ, who is without sin, commanded that Joshua be clothed in righteousness. Christ, the Son of God, made Joshua (Jesus) free from sin and clothed in priestly garments, including a turban. Under the old covenant, the high priest must wear a turban on his head.

Please note the command of the Angel of the LORD to Joshua, who stands in proxy for all the chosen people. He said to Joshua, and by proxy to us who are being rescued, "If you will walk in My ways [that is, remain faithful] and perform My service, then you will also govern My house and have charge of My courts, and I will give you free access [to My presence] among these who are standing here." (Zech. 3:7) This right of access is what was stripped from Satan and given back to us through Jesus Christ. So, in Christ, we will also govern over the house and courts of the LORD. This is why the scriptures say we will reign with Jesus: Joshua, who is our high priest for all eternity. The apostle Paul also alluded to this when he said, "that we are to judge angels" (1 Cor. 6:3).

The next verse (verse eight) is a foretelling of a new beginning. The LORD and the Son, or in this case, the Angel of the LORD now speaks as one foretelling the coming of the BRANCH: the Messiah, Who will put on the body prepared for Him as the man Jesus. And so, the Son, who is the BRANCH, and the Stone having seven eyes is to incarnate in bodily form as Jesus the Christ.

> "Now listen, Joshua, the high priest, you and your colleagues who are sitting in front of you—indeed they are men who are a symbol [of what is to come]—for behold, I am going to bring in My servant the Branch [in Messianic glory]. For behold, the stone which I have set before Joshua; on that one stone are seven eyes (symbolizing infinite intelligence, omniscience). Behold, I will engrave an inscription on it," declares the Lord of hosts, "and I will remove the wickedness and guilt of this land in a single day" (Zech. 3:8–9 AMP).

In verse nine, we see the Father: the LORD of Host, declaring that in one day, He will remove the iniquity of the land. That day was the day Jesus Christ, hanging on the cross, bowed His head and said, "It is finished." (Joh. 19:30) By this very act Satan, the accuser lost his right and authority to accuse the chosen people of the LORD.

All who are in Jesus, in Joshua, are free from condemnation. Therefore, the scripture says, "Who shall bring a charge against God's elect? It is God who justifies. Who is he who condemns? It is Christ who died, and furthermore is also risen, who is even at the right hand of God, who also makes intercession for us" (Rom. 8:33–34 NKJV)

God has spoken! Who can nullify it? The LORD rebuked Satan the accuser, period. Satan must keep his accusations to himself because he cannot bring them before the LORD God. He was kicked out of heaven into the earthly realm. So, he wants to make war with the chosen, but we overcome because of the blood of the Lamb, the price of our sins and redemption, and by the word of our testimony : (Rev. 12:11) our acceptance of Jesus Christ as Lord and Savior.

Embrace Your Worship of God!

The Father is seeking those who will worship Him in spirit and in truth, regardless of our present temporary sufferings or even our present jubilance. Good, bad, or evil events will come and go in our lives, but we must remain faithful in our worship of God. Even when we are hurt by those closest to us, family and friends alike, we cannot allow such pain to steal our right and privilege of worshipping the Father. We must embrace worshipping God as an integral part of our very existence. In the scriptures, we read where Jesus is talking to the woman at the well and told her, "The hour is coming, and is now here, when the true worshippers will worship the Father in spirit and truth, for the Father is seeking such people to worship him. God is spirit, and those who worship him must worship in spirit and truth" (John 4:22-24 ESV).

In order to worship the Father, we must know Him, and we know Him by believing in Christ Jesus, Whom the Father has sent. When we come to know Him, He changes our heart. This change that occurs within our heart is akin to the circumcision under the old covenant that identified a man as being a Jew in covenant relationship with God. Under this new covenant, God circumcised our hearts, thereby allowing us to worship Him in truth. Worship is not merely the bellowing of praises to God. Our hearts and lives must be truly devoted to God. Worship must be a lifestyle of faith, service, intimacy, Spirit filled praises and adoration to God.

Sacrifice has always been a major factor of worship. Therefore, when we forsake our own will and ways to fully give ourselves to God, we are offering to Him ourselves as a living sacrifice. This is true worship, to give one's heart and self completely to God. The scriptures speak of those who merely bellow praises with their lips. "These people draw near to Me with their mouth, and honor Me with their lips, but their heart is far from Me. And in vain they worship Me, Teaching as doctrines the commandments of men" (Matt. 15:8–9 NKJV). If we do not sacrifice our own will and ways to obey the commandments of God, then our worship is in vain.

The true worshippers are not practicing their own doctrine nor the teachings of men but are practicing the teachings of Christ, which fulfill the commandments of God the Father. So, under this new covenant, what are the teachings of Christ that fulfill the commandments of God? Jesus says that all the commandments hang on the first two. "Jesus said to him, 'You shall love the Lord your God with all your heart, with all your soul, and with all your mind.' This is the first and great commandment. And the second is like it: 'You shall love your neighbor as yourself.' On these two commandments hang all the Law and the Prophets" (Matt. 22:37–40 NKJV).

Therefore, under this new covenant, the fulfillment of all the requirements of the laws and prophets having been accomplished through Jesus Christ, our responsibility is to love God above all and love one another as He has loved us. Jesus said, "A new commandment I give to you, that you love one another; as I have loved you, that you also love one another. By this all will know that you are My disciples, if you have love for one another" (John 13:34–35 NKJV).

Living in a love relationship with God and loving people as He has loved us is in keeping with His commandments and is also a lifestyle of sacrificial worship of the Father. When we are practicing true worship, having our heart circumcised and keeping His commands, worship in the spirit becomes acceptable. We allow our spirit to rejoice in God as we sing psalms, hymns, give praises, thanksgivings, and glorifying God and Jesus Christ. We also offer up prayers, supplications, and requests to God concerning His will for our society, leaders, neighbors' friends, family, and ourselves.

Our Helper, the Holy Spirit, also joins us in these acts of worship so that we enter the most holy presence of God and Christ. The union of the Holy Spirit with our spirit assures us that our worship is well pleasing to God. Sometimes we begin praising God with our lips, but then the Holy Spirit will help us to shift and enter Spirit-filled worship that produces a well pleasing aroma to God. Under the old covenant, when meat offering was sacrificed to God, the aroma of it went up to God and was pleasing to Him. Likewise, our worship should produce an aroma that attracts God's attention.

Another part of our worship is meditation. There are times when we need to be still and know that He is God. (Ps.46:10) This means that we take the time to reflect on His goodness, mercy, forgiveness, creation, steadfast love toward us, His promises, and providence. We are to meditate on all the wonders and awesomeness of God. This is also often the time when the Lord will reveal more of Himself to us. When we contemplate the wonders of God, as though we are searching for hidden treasures, He allows us to find treasures within Him. In Proverbs, we read, "It is the glory of God to conceal a matter, But the glory of kings is to search out a matter" (Prov. 25:2 NKJV). In Christ, we are kings and priests of God. Therefore, it is to our glory when we search for the hidden treasure of God. Meditation is a part of worship that allows us to contemplate the wonders of God.

Our entire lives and lifestyles must become a sacrifice of true worship in spirit and in truth. Our fellowship with the body of Christ, which is the church, is another part to our acts of worship. It is the Father's will that we have cooperate worship and fellowship. Everything that Jesus did was to accomplish the will of the Father. Jesus, before His death on the cross, prayed that we, His disciples, would be one, just as He and His Father are One. Our worship and fellowship together as one body of believers is a testament to the world that we are Christ's disciples and that the Father sent Him into the world.

Jesus prayed not only for the apostles of that time but also for the believers of today. He secured the right for us to worship Him and fellowship with each other as one body of believers. The scripture records Jesus's prayer to the Father, saying, "I do not pray for these alone, but also for those who will believe in Me through their word; that they all may be one, as You, Father, are in Me, and I in You; that they also may be one in Us, that the world may believe that You sent Me." (John 17:20–-21NKJV)Furthermore, the scriptures also tell us to, "Consider one another in order to stir up love and good works, not forsaking the assembling of ourselves together, as is the manner of some, but exhorting one another, and so much the more as you see the Day approaching" (Heb. 10:24-25NKJV).

This assembling together should not be interpreted to mean only mass gatherings in a church building or temple. The church is not and never will be a building made by man's hands. God's people, human beings, are the temple of God and the body of believers. Remember that it is also written, "For where two or three are gathered together in My name, I am there in the midst of them" (Matt. 18:20 NKJV). Therefore, the assembling together of the body could be three people or three thousand people coming together to edify, sharpen, and strengthen one another in Christ.

Growing in Prayer Worship

Last, but not least, one of the most important aspects in worshiping the Father is praying or communicating with Him. As with any relationship, communication is a key aspect of growing in intimacy with God. Intimacy has been a great challenge for me over the years. I have a tendency of being antisocial, so, speaking and communicating is not my strong suit. I am the kind of person to go straight to the point. Because of this, I sometimes neglect the moments in prayer, that calls for stillness and quietness to just listen, for what God is saying. Praying and communicating with the Father, is a vital part of our ability to grow from glory to glory and develop intimacy with God.

Over the years, I have learned to view prayer and praying, perhaps a little differently from most people. I am consistently in communication or prayers with the Father, Son, and Holy Spirit. Many years ago, the Lord gave me two passages of scripture, that has guided my prayer life with God. The first scripture is found in Hebrews. The Lord showed me a long time ago, that I am never alone in this journey of life.

But you have come to Mount Zion and to the city of the living God, the heavenly Jerusalem, to an innumerable company of angels, to the general assembly and church of the firstborn who are registered in heaven, to God the Judge of all, to the spirits of just men made perfect, to Jesus the Mediator of the new covenant, and to the blood of sprinkling that speaks better things than that of Abel. (Heb. 12:22-24)

On the surface, these verses do not have anything to do with prayer or praying. However, what Jesus spoke into my heart, concerning these verses, is what keeps me in consistent communion with Him. He told me that He is my first and ever abiding company. The underlying theme of these verses is that we have **come to**, the city of the living God, to an innumerable company of angels, to God the judge of all, to Jesus our Mediator. (Heb. 12:22-24) The Lord revealed to me, that He is always with me, in every situation and that I can forever abide in His presence. Like the three Hebrew boys, in the fiery furnace, Jesus was with them even before they were thrown into the furnace. (Dan. 3:17)

Think for a moment, how long can you remain in the presence of someone without saying a word? If we truly believe that He is with us, then we will be more app to speak to Him and share Him with others. I have learned to engage God in continuous communication, praying, and at times making supplications and intercession. By no means, am I perfect, or better than anyone else. I keep learning and growing each day. Also, there are other times, in our devotion together, that He takes me into deeper prayer and intercession. The Holy Spirit sometimes takes over and intercedes on behalf of others. So, I walk and talk with God, just as I would with someone sitting beside me.

The other scripture, that has guided my prayer life, is the prayer of Abraham's servant, most likely Eliezer of Damascus, who was sent to find a wife for Abraham's son Isaac.

> Then the servant took ten of his master's camels and departed, taking all sorts of choice gifts from his master; and he arose and went to Mesopotamia1 to the city of Nahor. And he made the camels kneel down outside the city by the well of water at the time of evening, the time when women go out to draw water. And he said, "O Lord, God of my master Abraham, please grant me success today and show steadfast love to my master Abraham. Behold, I am

standing by the spring of water, and the daughters of the men of the city are coming out to draw water. Let the young woman to whom I shall say, 'Please let down your jar that I may drink,' and who shall say, 'Drink, and I will water your camels'—let her be the one whom you have appointed for your servant Isaac. By this I shall know that you have shown steadfast love to my master." Before he had finished speaking, behold, Rebekah, who was born to Bethuel the son of Milcah, the wife of Nahor, Abraham's brother, came out with her water jar on her shoulder. (Gen. 24:10-15 ESV)

Here, we have the servant of Abraham going about his master's business. He then made a simple request to the God of Abraham and God answered immediately. This answer that the servant needed, was necessary to fulfill God's plan and purpose for the linage of Abraham. There is no record, that this servant had any deep relationship with God, other than the fact that he was circumcised by Abraham. He was simply a servant, under covenant relationship with God, through circumcision and his master Abraham.

The servant was engaged in doing the business of his master Abraham and by default God's business. I came to learn from this servant, that God's answer to prayers, is not based on our eloquent words or the length of our prayers. God's response to our prayers, is based on relationship with Him, His kingdom purposes, and whether our prayers are focused on the fulfillment His business first.

First, we need be in a covenant relationship with God. Thank God for Jesus Christ, Who through His atoning blood sacrifice, has secured our covenant relationship with God. Just like Abraham's servant, we are the servants of Christ. We came into covenant relationship with God because of our master Jesus Christ. Therefore, in conducting the business of Christ, the assignment or calling that He has committed us, we can ask the Father, on the authority of Christ, for whatever is needed to accomplish His business.

The second premise of God's response to our prayer, is whether our prayers are aligned with His kingdom purposes. The servant was not seeking his desires, but the business of his master and by extension God's kingdom. If our prayers are selfish and self-serving, they may not be in alignment with God's plans and purposes.

When we consider God's purpose, there is an element of time associated with its fulfillment. If we are asking for something, before the proper timing on God's calendar, the outcome may be delayed until the proper time. Note that Abraham's servant, was at the right place and that it was the right time for Isaac to be married, for the fulfilment of God's plans, for the linage of Abraham. This crucial marriage was to fulfil both the current and future purposes of God, for the birth of the Christ and eternal life for mankind. The servant was not only at the right place, and at the right time, but he rightly prayed for the means to fulfil his assignment, which ultimately fulfilled

God's purpose and plans for mankind. This is why Christ Jesus teaches us to first pray for God's Kingdom and will to be done. (Mat. 6:10)

This brings us to the third premise of God's answer to prayers. Jesus said for us to pray for God's will to be done. (Mat. 6:10) In other words, whose will or whose business are we seeking when we pray. The servant was in the very act of carrying out the business or will of his master Abraham. If Jesus is our Lord and Master, we must prioritize our life and prayers to be about fulfilling His business.

We ought to seek first His kingdom business before praying about our own desires. (Mat. 6:33) However, it is not just a matter of words, the very actions in which we are engaged, must be in alignment with the business to which He has assigned us. When we are engaged in doing what He told us to do, God will answer our request even before we finish asking. Also, His answer will be in accordance with His timing, for fulfilling that portion of His plans on earth.

Spending time in prayer and communication with God, allows us to grow in intimacy with Him. Remember that communication is both hearing and speaking. A part of intimacy is keenly listening for His every word of instruction, comfort, and love. As we get to know Him more, we can discern better how He is moving in our life and the lives of others. Therefore, we can develop a better understanding of how to pray, concerning His will and our necessities for the accomplishment of His business.

In our prayer time, we will learn to check our hearts and examine our motives. Growing in prayer is an ongoing act of worship, service, and intimacy with God. There are many scriptures about prayer and praying, but these are some principles that the Lord has given to me in my prayer life of worship.

Growing in His Grace, Purpose, & Assignment

It is very important to know and understand your purpose or assignment in Christ. But even when you don't know it or understand it, the Sovereign God is the one Who orchestrates His plan for your life. Many would have you believe that you're only being used by God if you're doing something in the church or to be seen by the church. But God has His own plan for each and every one of us, and most of the time, it is not within the church building. The church is the entire body of Christ and not just those who are attending or assembling in a church building.

I was fifteen years old when the Lord baptized me with the Holy Spirit. It was over the summer prior to my high school years because I had completed the ninth grade in junior high school. I started high school in the tenth grade at George Westinghouse. While in high school, the opportunity raised for me to be a part of the Christian Culture Club overseen by Mr. Rosado. He was a faithful servant of God who encouraged us to seek and pursue after God. We gathered for praise and worship in his classroom. There we were beating drums on the tables, clapping, and singing, giving glory to God. Most of our time was spent searching the scriptures filled with excitement over every word of truth revealed to us. We were like treasure hunters finding jewels every place we dug. But we didn't keep our treasures hidden because we were too excited to contain it.

We witnessed and prayed with students, especially in the lunchroom. At times, we had more than twenty students worshipping God at the after-school meetings. We visited churches and ministered with them. We rode the subways and ministered to people, giving out tracts and praying for them. I remember one time we met in the park on a basketball court with Jose Collazo to worship and witness. I was very excited when he called me to the mic to say something to the people. I don't remember what I was supposed to say, but what came out of my mouth was "Jesus is alive and well." We all just kind of giggled about it and continued what was supposed to be done.

During my senior year of high school, I recall standing at the top of the staircase in the hallway and saying to God that I wanted to come back into the school system and give students what He had given me. It was strange because prior to that point, I had never thought about teaching and wanted only to build and fly planes. Although I started college for aeronautical engineering, the Lord brought me back into the school system. This was my assignment and how the Lord chose to use me. I would have never chosen teaching, especially in this capacity, if it had not been God-orchestrated.

From the onset of my assignment, God was showing me favor. Although I have always struggled with the English subject because of my native dialect, I managed to pass the exams. There were others who were more proficient than me in English, and they didn't pass. Also, for the interview after the test, I was called away from everyone else as we were all moving to another floor. I don't think it was that my answers were very exceptional, but I made it through all the requirements. This was nothing but the favor of God moving in my life and orchestrating my destiny.

I've spent the last thirty-five plus years within the NYC school system imparting the Word of God to many children amidst my duties as a teacher. I started teaching at age nineteen as an assistant teacher or substitute via apprenticeship (SVA). The first five years of my training and teaching were extremely challenging for me. There were many times I walked across the Brooklyn Bridge and thought about jumping. Everything in my life was happening so fast, and I didn't know how to handle it.

After attaining my permanent certification to teach Dental Laboratory Assisting, I was transferred from Westinghouse High School to teach at Clara Barton High School for health professions.

For approximately ten years, I was a part of and eventually ran the Christian Seekers Club in Clara Barton High School. Our main focus in the club was studying the Bible, prayer, and praise and worship. At one point, we designed a T-shirt for the group that read: Why Walk Alone When You Can Walk With Jesus. Although I've struggled in my walk with God at times, I've never stopped being available to give a word of encouragement to students who asked or showed interest in knowing more about God.

In the midst of a school environment where God and the Bible seemed to not be welcome, God had strategically positioned me to impact the lives of many. During the time of 9/11, when people were turning back to God, I was the one the principal called on to pray. However, since they knew my faith and in whose name I would pray, they had me write the prayer, which was delivered by a Jewish colleague, omitting the name of Jesus.

At the end of the Covid pandemic, the Lord showed me in a dream that I needed to take the vaccine and return to work. As the church administrator for OACM, I had already written the religious exemption letter used by some members of the church. But as for me, God said to take the vaccine. In my dream, He show me five students who were in a battlefield, and I was an exhausted soldier showing them how to fight and survive. Upon my return to work that fall, I had five students in my dental class to start with. During that school year, four students gave their lives to Christ, and the following year, one more student gave their life to Christ. These are just some examples of the work Father did through me during my assignment in the school system. As my assignment draws to a close, my prayer is for the fruits of my labor who have given their lives to God, that they will remain in Christ.

Another important point of worshipping the Father is to worship Him for who he is and all that he has done for us. I can recall February 2021, I was fasting for a few days, and I had some severe bowel movements at the time. I am not trying to be gross, but I just want to tell it as it occurred. I went to the bathroom, and I could not get up from the toilet. I called my wife, Dara-Ayo, and told her that I could not move, and I probably needed something in my system because my body was very weak. My wife went to the kitchen to prepare something for me to eat. I got up from the toilet, washed my hands, turned, and opened the door from the bathroom to the hallway. All I remember thereafter is that I was feeling very lightheaded. According to my wife, Dara, I fell out and smacked my head against the wall and fell to the floor. I don't know if I was just knocked out or if I was dead, but I can only report the facts to you as I recall and as my wife told me.

When I fell out, I was in another world walking down what seemed like a brick-paved road through some town. There were people in the buildings alongside the road, and I was a child again between eight and twelve years old. As I was walking down the road, I kept hearing a voice calling me, so I turned around and looked behind, and there was pitch darkness behind me. But as the voice called me, I was pulled back through the darkness and into my body again. I found myself flat on my face, and I was soaked and wet because apparently, I had peed all over myself. I heard my wife praying and crying, asking why I got up. "Why didn't you wait for me to help you?"

At this point, I came to my senses, and she helped me move to the couch to sit down. I was still very lightheaded, and sitting on the couch wasn't working, so she helped me get to the bedroom, where I lay down. My face was all scratched up, and it seemed as though I was dead for a short time.

My wife called my brother, who instructed her to take me to the hospital. She also called my pastor, then Pastor Wimberly, and she came over to help my wife. So, we all went to the emergency room where I was admitted for a day. They ran all kinds of tests, but everything seemed to be okay. In that short moment during my fasting and seeking God, my life could have been taken from me that quickly. So, I give God thanks and praise that I can stand today alive and well with the ability to use my breath to give him glory.

Shortly after this, in March of the same year, I had Covid and came near to the point of death again. If it had not been for the second doctor at the clinic who decided to give me some steroids, antibiotics, or whatever he gave me, I probably would not have been here to be writing this book. So, with every day, with each breath we take, we must learn to give thanks to the living God and honor him for his goodness and mercy toward us.

The Bible says the steadfast love of the Lord never ceases, and His mercies never come to an end. (Lam. 3:22) They are new every morning. Great is the faithfulness of our God. So, when I look back on the years of my life, many troubles at different times through which God saved my life, I cannot help but to give God praise, to thank him with all my heart, and to glorify his name.

I can also recall another time earlier in my life, during a period when my wife and I were going through marital struggles. One night at some point after 10 p.m., we were arguing. I became so angry that I jumped in my car and left to go to Buffalo from Staten Island, New York. I have never driven that fast in my life, and since then, I don't think I've ever driven that fast. I remember coming off Route 17 near Interstate 390 or someplace along there. I must've fallen asleep. All I remember is that approximately ten miles or so up the road, I woke up, going around this deep bend exit off the expressway. I recall going around the bend and waking up, traveling more than sixty miles an hour, and I came within feet of hitting the wall when I woke up. I was confused and didn't know where I was. I turned around and tried to backtrack to find where I was.

As I drove in the opposite direction, I kept looking along the roads, looking to find my body, thinking that maybe I was in my spirit and my body was lying on the road someplace. Truly I don't know how I got to that place from where I last remembered I was. Nevertheless, I managed to get back to a place where I knew where to go from there. So, from there, I continued my way to Buffalo to see my brother Winston.

At this point, it must have been 2 o'clock in the morning or very early morning, so the roads were empty. When I started on the 90 W. Buffalo straightaways, I started driving at about 125 mph. Thank God for saving my life. When I arrived at my brother's place, he scolded me for driving so foolishly, not realizing that one false move or my tire could've blown out, and that could've been the end.

Whatever years God gives me as I continue forward with my life, I'll choose to use my breath, my life, my body, my talent, and my resources to glorify God and serve Him the best way that I can. The Lord God is worthy of all praises! He's worthy of all the glory, all the honor, and all the power. There is no one else like God: awesome in power, loving kindness, merciful, and forgiving God. Blessed be the name of the Lord. It's no wonder the psalmist says, "Bless the Lord, oh my soul, and all that is within me, bless his Holy name. Bless the Lord, oh my soul, and forget not all his benefits." (Ps. 103: 1-2)

We worship God because the Lord, our God, is worthy of our worship, because he is the one and only true God. I share these testimonies here to demonstrating why we are to worship God and how we are to worship God throughout our lives. Also, through the sharing of our testimonies, we grow stronger and stronger. Hearing the testimonies of others helps us to grow from strength to strength and from glory to glory, knowing that God is faithful and that he will carry us through to the very end. As He has said, never shall He leave us nor forsake us. (Hew. 13:5)

Embrace Your Freedom!

There's a section in the scriptures where Jesus spoke about us being free. In this life and in our societies, the word freedom is used mostly in a relative sense. After all, how can we have freedom when there are so many levels of authorities that seem to control our very existence? There's also so much injustice, prejudices, racism, and control mechanisms, and to top it off, there is death and taxes. The world is also filled with prideful people who are always comparing themselves with each other. Therefore, they seem to be constantly engaged in competing for attention, recognition, kudos, and just being puffed up by each other.

Sadly, this has also become a part of the culture in the church community. If freedom is not found in our prideful ways, how do we find freedom in our society today? At best, it would seem like we can have relative freedom and not absolute freedom. But what is this freedom that Jesus Christ spoke about, and how does that impact our lives?

During the time Christ lived in the earth on assignment from the Father, many of the religious leaders were frustrated with him. Jesus was always about taking care of Father's business, and the religious leaders could not understand why he was not about practicing religion like they did. Too often in the church today, as it was then, believers are going about seeking honor and applauds from each other. Therefore, there is always the tendency to perform for each other to be accepted as one anointed and approved. But from who are we seeking this approval?

When Christ did a miracle, healed the sick, cast out demons, and many other acts, he sounded no trumpets for attention, quite the opposite. He wanted to remain anonymous but for the recipients of the miracles to give Father the praise. Too often in today's church, many are trumpeting their résumé of accomplishments in a way that gives the appearance that the purpose is for their own honor applauds. This type of behavior creates a culture in the church where many are more focused on putting on a performance. There is a freedom that comes in seeking only to please God. There is the freedom of not having to perform and just being genuine in service to God and others.

When my wife and I would go to different churches, we were often faced with opposition from some who couldn't receive our pure motives. We have always served God and others wholeheartedly and without any hidden agenda. What we had truly longed for the most was to be taught in the teachings of Christ. Being hungry for God and to find our purpose people usually either tried to sabotage or elevate us perhaps too quickly. But all we wanted was to learn in order to fulfill our purpose in the body of Christ. The Lord desires for us to have complete freedom from sin, which includes pride in order that we can live humble in His service.

Another aspect of this freedom has to do with who we truly are as is evident by our actions. Our actions give insight into who truly rules in our hearts. In the book of John, the scripture records a discourse between Jesus and the Jews about being free.

> *Jesus said to the Jews who had believed him, "If you abide in my word, you are truly my disciples, and you will know the truth, and the truth will set you free." They answered him, "We are offspring of Abraham and have never been enslaved to anyone. How is it that you say, 'You will become free'?" Jesus answered them, "Truly, truly, I say to you, everyone who practices sin is a slave to sin. The slave does not remain in the house forever; the son remains forever. So, if the Son sets you free, you will be free indeed. I know that you are offspring of Abraham; yet you seek to kill me because my word finds no place in you. I speak of what I have seen with my Father, and you do what you have heard from your father." They answered him, "Abraham is our father." Jesus said to them, "If you were Abraham's children, you would be doing the works Abraham did, but now you seek to kill me, a man who has told you the truth that I heard from God. This is not what Abraham did. You are doing the works your father did." They said to him, "We were not born of sexual immorality.*

> *We have one Father—even God." Jesus said to them, "If God were your Father, you would love me, for I came from God and I am here. I came not of my own accord, but he sent me. Why do you not understand what I say? It is because you cannot bear to hear my word. You are of your father the devil, and your will is to do your father's desires. He was a murderer from the beginning, and does not stand in the truth, because there is no truth in him. When he lies, he speaks out of his own character, for he is a liar and the father of lies"* (John 8:31–44 ESV).

In this discourse, we see Jesus speaking to this crowd not only about freedom but about the way in which we can have freedom. Freedom is connected to our way of living, and our way of living is connected to whom we belong to or the system to which we yield ourselves. Jesus said that if we abide in His Word, not only will we be His disciples, but we will also know the Truth and be made free. In other words, by getting to know Him and living in accordance with His Word, we are made free. This freedom goes much deeper than what appears on the surface. First of all, Jesus is speaking to the fact that we are ultimately slaves to what we obey or the things we give ourselves over to. He is linking freedom all the way back to the beginning, where Adam and Eve gave themselves over to Satan by becoming obedient to that devil.

Jesus said that whoever commits, or, in other words, practice sin is a slave to sin. So, whenever we live in sinful disobedience to the life-giving Word of God, we make ourselves slaves to sin, leading to unhealthy habits, addictions, bondage, and ultimately death. The responses of the crowd clearly let us know that they were only wise to or concerned with their physical connections. They uttered, "We are Abraham's children!"

This brings us to the second point of Jesus's discourse with them. Freedom is not granted based on biological factors or worldly systems but rather by our spiritual connection. It is clear that all that this world has to offer cannot and has not made anyone free. Even the most wealthy, privileged, and powerful are subject to sickness, death, and, yes, taxes. Furthermore, we are all subject to the great judgment after death. But Jesus spoke of freedom from the very source of the reason for our suffering, injustices, prejudices, and even death. The source of all the pain and suffering in the world is a direct result of our lustful ways, pridefulness, disobedience, lies, and all our sinful ways. The world has produced for us the fruits of our own actions.

Jesus spoke of freedom from the one who can hold you a prisoner of the world systems, sin, and death. Jesus made a statement, saying that it is the spirit that gives life; the flesh profits nothing (see John 6:63). In other words, the body without the spirit is dead. However, we live our lives more concerned about our bodies than we are about our spirit. Because of this, we strive for physical freedom yet not understanding that if our spirit man is not free, we can never obtain freedom. On another level, you can also say that if one is not free internally, he or she is not free externally. But Jesus spoke of freedom on an even deeper level than our mental and emotional wellbeing.

The freedom of our spirit is entirely based on our spiritual lineage. In other words, who is your father? If you are born again in Jesus Christ, then God is your heavenly Father, and you are free from the power of sin and death. If God is not your heavenly Father, then you remain under the control of sin, death, and the powers of darkness.

Jesus is clearly letting this crowd know that their actions and thoughts, for that matter, testify as to who is their father. It is also clear that the crowd understood what Jesus was saying. Namely, if God is your Father, you are free, but if the devil is your father, you remain a slave to sin. Jesus says the slave does not abide in the house forever, but the Son abides forever.

What does this discourse have to do with us and our freedom? I grew up in a religious societal mindset that was very unforgiving toward sin in our lives. I was taught or led to believe that the moment you sin, you lose your salvation, and you need to be saved all over again. While it is true that when we sin, we are acting like and being influenced by the devil, it is equally true that our God is a forgiving God. Because of the grace and freedom that Father has given us, we can repent, get up again, and keep waking with Him. It is not Father's will for us to be subject to a weight of rule, dos, and don'ts, as though we are under the "Law." It is His will that we walk in the "royal law of liberty and love." We are to love Him above all, and we are to love one another as He has loved us. This is a part of our freedom in Christ, not that we should sin but that we should live an abundant life. As the scripture says, "For this is the will of God, that by doing good you may put to silence the ignorance of foolish men—as free, yet not using liberty as a cloak for vice, but as bondservants of God" (1 Pet. 2:15–16 NKJV).

Most of the time, we are far too sin-focused instead of being love-centered and liberty-minded. We point our fingers at those who fall almost to the point of crucifying them with our looks, words, and actions. We forget that Christ died for them and that His grace is sufficient for us all. Even those in the world who are practicing their sinful ways, some in the church persist in condemning them. This culture creates a hostile climate in the body of Christ so that those who are believers quiver at the thought of making an error. On account of this, believers who have fallen hide and cover up their mistakes, unable to be free from it because of the fear of condemnation and shame. This hostile culture is not of God!

Let us remember that Jesus said that Father did not send Him into the world to condemn the world. He also said that in the same manner that the Father sent Him, He has sent us into the world not to condemn but that they might be saved. (See John 3:17; 20:21). Furthermore, concerning the believer, let us not forget that Jesus has broken down the dividing wall of hostility that kept all people, both Jew and Gentile, separated from Him, making peace for us all. Consider the following scripture!

> *But now in Christ Jesus you who once were far off have been brought near by the blood of Christ. For he himself is our peace, who has made us both one and has broken down in his flesh the dividing wall of hostility by abolishing the law of commandments expressed in ordinances, that he might create in himself one new man in place of the two, so making peace, and might reconcile us both to God in one body through the cross, thereby killing the hostility* (Eph. 2:13–16 ESV).

Why, then, should the church hold to such a hostile, unforgiving, and untrusting climate? Such behavior only hinders believers from coming out of the dark, confessing and repenting of their sins. I am not saying that we should condone sin of any kind. Father does not condone sin, and neither do I. The scripture clearly says, "For you were called to freedom, brothers. Only do not use your freedom as an opportunity for the flesh, but through love serve one another" (Gal. 5:13 ESV). So, why, then, do we often find ourselves so laden down with sin and for years even struggling to be free?

The first reason is the hostile culture that has been in the church, where we shoot our wounded instead of nursing them back to health. The second reason is that we are ignorant of or have forgotten the provisions that Christ has established for us when we fall. It is written, "My little children, I am writing these things to you so that you may not sin. But if anyone does sin, we have an advocate with the Father, Jesus

Christ the righteous. He is the propitiation for our sins, and not for ours only but also for the sins of the whole world" (1 John 2:1–2 ESV).

Jesus gave us the example of feet washing to follow. Very few people in the churches I have attended talk about feet washing anymore. Jesus washed His disciples' feet, even the feet of Judas, who betrayed Him. I believe His example of feet washing is a message for us today so that the church can be without spot or wrinkles.

In the days Jesus walked on earth, there was a long-established culture of providing water for you and your guests to wash their feet upon entering your home. During those times, sandals were the main covering for the feet. No matter how much you washed as soon as you walked outside, your feet would get dirty. So, Jesus said, "The one who has bathed does not need to wash, except for his feet, but is completely clean . . ." (John 13:10 ESV). If you read the entirety of this chapter in the book of John, Jesus is using a physical common-sense activity to teach a deeper spiritual principle. We have been made clean because of Jesus Christ, and we are clothed in His righteousness. However, as we live or walk in this world our feet will get dirty. None of us are capable within ourselves of living a completely sinless life. So, it is more so a matter of when you sin.

It is Father's will for us to wash each other's feet. This is not in the physical sense of using soap and water to wash our feet but rather that we ought to have a humble heart for helping those who have fallen into diverse situations of sin.

How is it that we want to rescue the lost souls and condemn the wounded saints?

Even in the world, there are provisions for those who struggle with addictions. But in the church, where are the hospitals and the ambulance service, spiritually speaking, to care for those who find themselves struggling with sin? "Jesus answered and said to them, 'Those who are well have no need of a physician, but those who are sick. I have not come to call the righteous, but sinners, to repentance'" (Luke 5:31–32 NKJV).

A part of my exercise routine is to walk around the complex in which I am living. Although it is paved and has sidewalks, there are sections where there is accumulated gravel and dirt on the ground. No matter how tightly I have my sneakers on, I still get gravel in my sneakers. Sometimes I try to ignore it, especially when I'm in a good groove and don't want to break my stride. But eventually, the gravel in my sneakers will begin to slow me down, and I must stop and clean the gravel from underneath my feet in the sneakers.

No matter how hard we try, no matter how perfect our stride in life is, we will get some gravel underneath our feet, and ignoring it only produces soreness. Eventually, that soreness can become bitterness, prideful, self-righteousness, and it may even become bloody and infectious. When such soreness becomes bloody or infectious, you begin to cause harm to yourself and others around you.

If one part of the body is sick, the whole body feels the pain and partakes in the suffering. Therefore, it is for the betterment of the whole church community that we seek to restore one another and show compassion to those who have become entangled with sinfulness. We are commanded to wash their feet by nursing them back to a healthy life in Christ. Jesus said, "If I then, your Lord and Teacher, have washed your feet, you also ought to wash one another's feet. For I have given you an example, that you also should do just as I have done to you" (John 13:14-15 ESV). If we become more forgiving, choosing not to expose, condemn, nor condone the sins of those who have been overtaken by sin, then they can come to true repentance. It is written, "And above all things have fervent love for one another, for "love will cover a multitude of sins" (1 Pet. 4:8 NKJV). Let us live by the royal law of love, embracing our freedom, and when we sin, have the supporting culture of forgiveness and love to help each other get back up again.

One God, One Body, & One Spirit!

Sometimes we focus more on doing things in the church than we do on becoming children of God. The scripture said to them who receive Him, He gives them the right to become children of God. The transformation process is not so much about what we do as much as it is about submitting to the Spirit that we become children of God. A part of our becoming children of God and our transformation is our unification in becoming one family of God. Jesus said, "I am the good shepherd; and I know My sheep and am known by My own. As the Father knows Me, even so I know the Father; and I lay down My life for the sheep. And other sheep I have which are not of this fold; them also I must bring, and they will hear My voice; and there will be one flock and one shepherd" (John 10:14–16 NKJV) It has always been Father's will that we should be ONE flock having ONE Shepherd, just as Christ and the Father are ONE. Woven throughout the scriptures is the message that there is ONE God whose will is to have ONE family of believers, guided by ONE Spirit: The Holy Spirit. Father has already prepared the way in Christ Jesus for this to happen. In John 17, we find Jesus praying concerning the church body for us to become perfectly one.

> *I have given them your word, and the world has hated them because they are not of the world, just as I am not of the world. I do not ask that you take them out of the world, but that you keep them from the evil one. They are not of the world, just as I am not of the world. Sanctify them in the truth; your word is truth. As you sent me into the world, so I have sent them into the world. And for their sake I consecrate myself, that they also may be sanctified in truth. I do not ask for these only, but also for those who will believe in me through their word, that they may all be one, just as you, Father, are in me, and I in you, that they also may be in us, so that the world may believe that you have sent me. The glory that you have given me I have given to them, that they may be one even as we are one, I in them and you in me, that they may become perfectly one, so that the world may know that you sent me and loved them even as you loved me* (John 17:14–23 ESV).

This is the most detailed recorded prayer of Jesus praying for us to the Father in His final days. If anybody's prayers are answered, Jesus's prayers are answered first. First, He identifies us as aliens to this world because of Father's Word abiding within us. Do you recognize yourself as being alien to this world? We are commanded to set our minds on the things above and not on the things of this world. Our focus should not be the American dream or the world's dream but the reality of becoming one with God in Christ! I'm not saying being equal to God but rather a oneness so that we become perfectly aligned with His will and directions.

Our becoming one family of God means that our will must give way to the will of the Father. Jesus was always about Father's business. He totally depended on hearing and speaking only the words given to Him by the Father. He said, "The word which you hear is not Mine but the Father's who sent Me." (Jn. 14:24 NKJV) He also said, praying to the Father, "I have given to them the words which You have given Me." (Jn. 17:8 NKJV) Our focus should never be to impress each other nor to embellish the Word of God. We must give the Word He has given to us. We must emulate Jesus and become totally submitted to the Spirit of Truth.

Jesus also was praying that, "They may all be one, just as you, Father, are in me, and I in you, that they also may be in us." (Jn. 17:21 NKJV) This prayer unfolds two priorities in our becoming one family of God. The first is that we must be one with each other. We must become one body, be of one heart, be of one Spirit, and be of one mind, with Jesus Christ being the head of us all. Can you even imagine the whole church body being one just the way that Jesus and the Father are one? Yet, this is what Jesus prayed for and also what the apostles understood. Consider and meditate on the following scriptures concerning the body of believers: the church.

> *Now the full number of those who believed were of one heart and soul, and no one said that any of the things that belonged to him was his own, but they had everything in common* (Acts 4:32 ESV).

> *If the whole body were an eye, where would be the sense of hearing? If the whole body were an ear, where would be the sense of smell? But as it is, God arranged the members in the body, each one of them, as he chose. If all were a single member, where would the body be? As it is, there are many parts, yet one body. The eye cannot say to the hand, 'I have no need of you,' nor again the head to the feet, 'I have no need of you'* (1 Cor. 12:17–21 ESV).

> *I, therefore, a prisoner for the Lord, urge you to walk in a manner worthy of the calling to which you have been called, with all humility and gentleness, with patience, bearing with one another in love, eager to maintain the unity of the Spirit in the bond of peace. There is one body and one Spirit—just as you were called to the one hope that belongs to your call— one God and Father*

of all, who is over all and through all and in all (Eph. 4:1–4, 6 ESV).

The scriptures tell us that the stories of those who were before us were written as an example for us to learn from. Consider the story of Joshua and the children of Israel when they fought against Ai and lost the battle. The scriptures tell us that they lost the battle because there was sin in the camp of Israel. In fact, it says that Israel had sinned.

> *So, the Lord said to Joshua: "Get up! Why do you lie thus on your face? Israel has sinned, and they have also transgressed My covenant which I commanded them. For they have even taken some of the accursed things and have both stolen and deceived; and they have also put it among their own stuff. Get up, sanctify the people, and say, 'Sanctify yourselves for tomorrow, because thus says the Lord God of Israel: "There is an accursed thing in your midst, O Israel; you cannot stand before your enemies until you take away the accursed thing from among you""'* (Josh. 7:10).

Three thousand men were sent to destroy what was relatively a small town in comparison to Jericho. They were defeated, and thirty-six people lost their lives because of the sin of one man. But was it only one man who had sinned? If you read the account of the entire chapter seven of Joshua, it was one man, Achan, who had done the sinful act, but God dealt with the entire nation as covenant breakers. God held them collectively and individually responsible.

The Jews understood this principle of being one in God. They understood that the sin of one person impacts the entire body of believers. Even in the time Jesus walked the earth, Caiaphas prophesied that it was better that one man should die for the people than for the entire nation to perish. (Jn. 11:49-51) The principle of our interconnectedness: ONE man, ONE family, ONE nation under ONE God is evident in how God dealt with Israel.

Furthermore, concerning dealing with the sin of Israel, Achan and everything under his authority had to be purged— cut off from Israel. Similarly, to the treatment of gangrene, Achan had to be surgically removed from the body of believers. Note that there are other treatments for gangrene that can restore the blood flow and save that member of the body.

Please note also that our "Joshua" is Jesus Christ, who works through the Holy Spirit. As it was with Ananias and Sapphira standing before Peter, the Holy Spirit is the ONLY ONE who cuts anyone off from the body of Christ!

Nevertheless, Joshua and the children of Israel had to purge the sin from the body of believers in order to win against "AI." What is "AI" about to do in our generation? Can we win our "AI" battle without being united as one body, pure and holy, before God? Christ is returning for a church without spot or wrinkle. He has already taken care of our sin issue. Can we come together as ONE body led by ONE Spirit and under

ONE LORD and King, who is Jesus Christ, the head of the church? Can we understand that our actions, individually and collectively, impact the entire body of believers? The impact of our actions affects us all, beginning with our own family and those under our authority, and spreads to the whole body.

The second priority in our becoming one family of God is being one with God in Christ. Jesus said that "The glory that you have given me I have given to them, that they may be one even as we are one, I in them and you in me, that they may become perfectly one." (Jn. 17:22 ESV) Again, I'm not saying equal to God but rather a oneness so that we become perfectly aligned with His will and directions.

Think of military soldiers marching. They are of different ranking and are therefore not the same in the office, but they march in lockstep with each other. God has shown us an example in the vision of the cherubs and the whirling wheels described by the prophet Ezekiel in chapter ten of that book. These were individual cherubs and separate whirling wheels but functioning as one unit. Consider this record of what Ezekiel witnessed and wrote about.

> *And their whole body, their rims, and their spokes, their wings, and the wheels were full of eyes all around—the wheels that the four of them had. As for the wheels, they were called in my hearing "the whirling wheels." And everyone had four faces: the first face was the face of the cherub, and the second face was a human face, and the third the*

> *face of a lion, and the fourth the face of an eagle. And when the cherubim went, the wheels went beside them. And when the cherubim lifted up their wings to mount up from the earth, the wheels did not turn from beside them. When they stood still, these stood still, and when they mounted up, these mounted up with them,* **for the spirit of the living creatures was in them** (Ezek. 10:12–emphasis added).

We must march in lockstep with the Holy Spirit. This means we must be led by the Spirit. The spirit of the living creatures was in the whirling wheels, so the wheels were one with them. The Holy Spirit of God is within us, and we must completely submit our will to Him so that we will be one with Him. Jesus was given the Spirit without measure, and He was led by the Spirit. Likewise, He has given us this glory so that we can be one with the Spirit and be led by the Spirit.

In Amos 3:3, the question is asked, how can two walk together unless they agreed? In other words, how can we walk with God if we're going in different directions? The only way we can have victory over our flesh is to walk or, rather, live in the Spirit. Be one with the Holy Spirit!

Moreover, Jesus is called Immanuel, meaning God with us. (Matt. 1:23) Jesus dwells within us, the Father dwells within us, and the Holy Spirit dwells within us forever! If we can envision ourselves as the whirling wheels in the report of Ezekiel and Christ being our head, then the Spirit of Christ operating in us makes us one with Him and keeps us in lockstep with Him. The Spirit of Christ is the Spirit of Truth and the same Holy Spirit of God the Father.

When we received Jesus Christ, we became children of God and therefore one family of God. However, there is still a process of transformation that must occur until we are like Him. The scripture says that it has not yet been revealed what we shall be, but when He is revealed, we shall be like Him (1 John 3:3). So, we don't fully know what we are going to be, but as we continue to submit to Him, He will bring us to perfection. Furthermore, the apostle Paul said, "Not that I have already attained, or am already perfected; but I press on, that I may lay hold of that for which Christ Jesus has also laid hold of me" (Phil. 3:12 NKJV). Therefore, as long as there is breath in us, we must keep pressing on toward obtaining the prize of the upward call of God in Christ.

Lifelong Application

As I said in the introduction, when I first gave my life to the Lord, there was no one there to really guide me and advise me on what it meant to walk with the Lord. I was young, fifteen years old, and I went about seeking girls because that's what boys at that age did. It was not until I was baptized in the Holy Spirit that my life really changed, and I began to live for God.

I am not sure of the time, but I believe that it was a Thursday evening or perhaps a Friday evening when my aunt Joyce invited me to go to church. At first, I resisted and told her that I was going to Kings Plaza to find girls. She then proceeded to tell me that I would find girls in church, so I went to church with her. I cannot tell you what the pastor and leaders were preaching about that night, but I can tell you what happened toward the ending of the service. I did not know anyone there except my aunt, and I recognized a distant family member who was the bishop of the church, Bishop Burris. He was also on stage with them.

The leadership on the pulpit began to make altar calls, and they were calling people to come and give their lives to the Lord. One of the leaders—I don't know the man—but he pointed directly at me and asked me to come forward, so I did. When

I reached the altar, he told me that I needed to give my life to the Lord. My replied to him was, "I have already given my life to the Lord." He then said to me that I needed to worship Him, and I needed to praise the Lord. Those words were like a foreign language to me; it was as though I had never heard those words before, and if I did, I cannot say where. However, he told me to lift my hands and praise the Lord, to which I was obedient. After I said "Praise the Lord" three times, everything changed in my life. After saying "Praise the Lord" the third time, I was in two different realms, which I never understood before, nor did I fully understand it then. What I am about to tell you at this point is what I experienced personally and what my aunt also told me was happening to me at the very same moment simultaneously.

After I said "Praise the Lord" the third time, I was no longer in the church building. I was up in the heavens far beyond the stars, looking down at the stars below my feet, and everything was pitch black except for the brightest light that was shining down from above me. I was standing with my head bowed down, my hands were clasped in front underneath my chin, and I was still saying, "Praise the Lord." A voice was speaking to me from the light, and the words that were spoken passed through me and went into my heart. I could literally see the words entering through me and into my heart, where they stayed. However, I could not understand what was being spoken to me. But I felt the greatest peace I've ever known, and I was perfectly still, feeling the warmth of the light shining down on me, and the voice continued to speak into my heart.

This is my account of what happened that night, and it was all that I was aware of that was taking place.

According to my aunt, I was rolling around on the floor and screaming, and their leadership was casting demons out of me. Money that was in my pocket fell out, and when she came up to pick up my money, they were calling her a thief. They did not know that I was with her, for, as I said, I didn't know anyone there. Afterward, when I was back in my body, they had me stand up, and I began to explain to them what had happened and what I had experienced. This was my experience of being baptized with the Holy Spirit.

From that day forward, my life changed, and I continue to live for God ever since that day. Yes, indeed, I have made many mistakes along the way, and I have fallen several times. However, the Spirit of God has never left me, and he continues to walk with me this day. As far as the changes I experienced thereafter, what they were and how they change my life is expressed in the following practical life applications that the Holy Spirit worked through me for me to grow in God.

Eat Well and Exercise!

After being baptized with the Holy Spirit, I was like a man who had been starving. I had such a hunger for the Word of God, so I spent hours at a time reading and studying the Word of God. I had bought myself a blue-covered leather-bound Bible. I carried it back and forth to school, and it seemed like every chance I got, I was reading it. This was a part of my accelerated growth in God.

As followers of Christ, reading and studying the Word of God is one of the most essential components for growing in our faith in Christ. Jesus said He is the living bread that comes down from heaven that we may eat and not be hungry or thirsty. He said that the words he speaks are spirit and life. He also stated that we should not live by the physical bread only but by every word that comes from the mouth of God. (Jn. 6:35-51) Consider the following scriptures and meditate on them.

> *"Jesus said to them, 'I am the bread of life; whoever comes to me shall not hunger, and whoever believes in me shall never thirst. Truly, truly, I say to you, whoever believes has eternal life. I am the bread of life. Your fathers ate the manna in the wilderness, and they died. This is the bread that*

comes down from heaven, so that one may eat of it and not die. I am the living bread that came down from heaven. If anyone eats of this bread, he will live forever. And the bread that I will give for the life of the world is my flesh'" (John 6:35, 47–51 ESV).

"It is the Spirit who gives life; the flesh profits nothing. The words that I speak to you are spirit, and they are life" (John 6:63 NKJV).

"But He answered and said, 'It is written, "Man shall not live by bread alone, but by every word that proceeds from the mouth of God"'" (Matt. 4:4 NKJV).

Any good nutritionist will tell us that to stay healthy and fit, we must eat right and exercise. So, it is also in the spiritual; we must feast on the Word of Life, and we must practice living by the Word, thereby exercising the Word in us. I don't know anyone, who starting out exercising can lift any amount of weight and run as long or as fast as they like. No one starts out being perfect at exercising, and even after years of exercising, it can still be a challenge. Why, then, do we insist on being perfect and beat up ourselves and each other for not doing everything right in our daily living for God? Just like beginning to exercise or a baby learning to crawl before being able to run, you will fall, and you will make mistakes. But you don't quit! Get back up, knowing that you are serving a forgiving God who understands your weaknesses. Know that living for Christ, reading, and studying the Word of God is a growing process. Know that Father is 100 percent committed to your being transformed to carry His glory.

Another thing that changed in my life after being baptized with the Holy Spirit is my desire and drive for worship. Accompanying my Bible was a small blue hymnal that my mother or my aunt Dorothy had sent to me. When I was not reading the Word, I was singing and praising God within myself. Yes, praising God within myself because most of the time, I was traveling on buses back and forth to school. I was living in Canarsie and traveling to downtown Brooklyn attending George Westinghouse High School.

Once again, consider the following scriptures.

> *"Don't be drunk with wine, because that will ruin your life. Instead, be filled with the Holy Spirit, singing psalms and hymns and spiritual songs among yourselves, and making music to the Lord in your hearts. And give thanks for everything to God the Father in the name of our Lord Jesus Christ"* (Eph. 5:18–20 NLT).

> *"Enter his gates with thanksgiving, and his courts with praise! Give thanks to him; bless his name! For the Lord is good; his steadfast love endures*

forever, and his faithfulness to all generations" (Ps. 100:4–5 ESV).

"For great is the Lord, and greatly to be praised; he is to be feared above all gods. For all the gods of the peoples are worthless idols, but the Lord made the heavens. Splendor and majesty are before him; strength and beauty are in his sanctuary. Ascribe to the Lord, O families of the peoples, ascribe to the Lord glory and strength! Ascribe to the Lord the glory due his name; bring an offering and come into his courts! Worship the Lord in the splendor of holiness; tremble before him, all the earth!" (Ps. 96:4–9 ESV).

When we are truly worshipping the Lord and from the depths of our being, that is, from our spirit, this worship is acceptable to God. How can we be sure of this? The Father is seeking true worshippers, those who will worship Him in spirit and in truth. The Holy Spirit will fill you and move you into even deeper depths of worship. By the presence of the Holy Spirit with you, you can be assured that your worship is accepted by Father.

Enough cannot be said about the work of the Holy Spirit in helping, leading, guiding, and instructing us in the way of Jesus Christ. If we engage in true worship, reading and studying the Word of God, and trying the best we can to live by it, the Holy Spirit is the one who will transform us. There is often too much emphasis on what we must do instead of allowing God through His Word and His Holy Spirit to do the transformation of our lives, making us more and more like Him.

Some Names of God & Helpful Terms

It is important to understand that the only language not created by God is lying. God created languages, and He understands all languages. Most importantly, He knows and understands our hearts way beyond our own capacity to understand our hearts. So, when it comes to the names of God, we should not feel compelled to use one or the other. In fact, Jesus said that when we pray, we should simply address God by saying Father in heaven. Jesus, who is our example, never referred to God using anything else but Father. The names of God are representative of His character and attributes.

Names of God

Elohim: Powerful God
Yehovah or Jehovah: Self-Existing or Eternal.
Jehovah Shalom: The LORD is Peace
Jehovah Rohi: The LORD is my Shepherd.
Jehovah Raphe: The LORD Heals
Jehovah Jireh: The LORD provides.
El Shaddai: Almighty God

There are so many more names, but these are some of my favorites.

Names of Jesus the Christ

Jesus or Jehoshua: Jehovah saved or brings salvation.
Christ: Anointed One or the Messiah
Immanuel: God with us

There are many other names and descriptions of Jesus, such as Lamb of God, King of kings, Word of God, Son of God, Prince of Peace, Advocate, Counselor, Teacher, Mighty God, and the list goes on.

Some Common Terms

The following definitions are either paraphrased or quoted from the webster dictionary.

The Holy Communion: A consecrated time for remembering the dead, burial, and resurrection of Jesus Christ by sharing symbolic bread representing His body that was broken and symbolic wine representing His blood of the new covenant that was shed for the remission of sins

Atonement/Atone: To make amends; to provide or serve as reparation or compensation for something bad or unwelcome: our sins (Merriam-Webster Dictionary)

Fasting: The abstaining from food and water for a time to humble oneself before God and promote spiritual growth (Merriam-Webster Dictionary)

Glory: This has many meanings, but here are three that should be helpful: 1.) worshipful praise, honor, and thanksgiving; 2.) something that secures praise or renown; and 3.) great beauty and splendor. (Merriam-Webster Dictionary)

Hell: The nether realm of the devil and the demons in which condemned people suffer everlasting punishment (Merriam-Webster Dictionary)

Rapture: To be taken up into heaven to be with the Lord for all eternity

Resurrection: To be raised from the dead and another reference of the power of Jesus Christ

The Tribulation: A time of the outpouring of God's wrath upon the earth

Salvation: Deliverance from the power and effects of sin and the wrath of God (Merriam-Webster Dictionary)

Saved: Delivered from sin and from spiritual death; rescued from eternal punishment (Merriam-Webster Dictionary)

Sojourn: A temporary stay or residence; think of this world as a hotel stopover on our journey into eternity with God. (Merriam-Webster Dictionary)

References

Strong, James. Strongs Exhaustive Concordance of the Bible. Crusade Bible Publishers, Inc. 1894

P.P. Bliss. Wonderful Words of Life. Church Hymnal, song #205. Tennessee Music and Printing Company, 1951

Merriam-Webster Dictionary APP. Merriam Webster, Inc. 2023